T0132441

Marlborough on My Mind

Other book by author: "The First Hundred Years"

Marlborough on My Mind

MaryLou Mahan

iUniverse, Inc.
New York   Bloomington

iUniverse books may be ordered through booksellers or by contacting:

iUniverse
1663 Liberty Drive
Bloomington, IN 47403
www.iuniverse.com
1-800-Authors (1-800-288-4677)

ISBN: 978-1-4401-4827-9 (sc)

Printed in the United States of America

iUniverse rev. date: 08/14/2009

Dedicated to my brother, Bob Hennekens,
who was always there for me.

Table of Contents

List of Illustrations

Thank you, thank you, thank you.....
To all who helped make this book possible - including, but not limited to:

Vin Russo; Gerhard Burfeindt; Betsy, Bill & Addison Wilklow; George Badner; Carol Ann Purtell; Al Rhodes; Richard & Sunny McMullen; Carol Felter; Bob Young; Pat Mackey; Sam Quimby and the Marlboro Yacht Club; Pat Favata and Crawford House; Bruno Ronkese; Glen Clarke and the Friends of the Milton-on-the-Hudson Railroad Station; Betsy McKean, Newburgh Records Management Officer; Emily Wiseman; Mel Alonge; Jack Baldwin; Mike Canosa; Adele Woolsey Lyons; The 53ers; Valeria Dawes Terwilliger; Jim Manion; Bill& Judy Gephard , Cathy Cosman and Jesse Elliott, Jr.

As is usually the case, the mistakes are my own. I only pray there are not many of them.

Of Education
The "Grand" Street School

Grand Street School
1888-1975

The site, on the northeast corner of Grand and Church Streets was purchased in 1888 from Matthew Berean. The residents of the hamlet of Marlboro, recognizing the need for more space for the growing number of students attending their schools, had decided on building a "new" school. The school was opened in December of 1888. At that time it had three finished rooms. The opening ceremonies were held in the "Principal's Room". There were so many in attendance, the room was filled to overflowing. The principal was a John Frost Harris. The building became known as "The Grand Street School".

On the first day of school there were 160 students in attendance. The faculty consisted of Principal Harris, whose charges were the advanced grades; Miss Cornelia Purdy, in charge of the intermediate

1

grades and Miss Rebecca Rusk, teacher for the primary grades. In 1895 Edward Baldwin became principal and the fourth room in the attic was opened and Miss Mary DuBois was hired as an additional teacher. Baldwin left Marlboro in 1900 and was followed by Arthur Ramsdell.

There were two additions to the original building which was in the Swiss style of architecture; one in 1904 and another in 1910. After the passage, by the community, of the necessary appropriations in 1904, a committee of seven townspeople headed by Dr. Palmer took charge of insuring the integrity of the addition. The addition consisted of adding to the north and west side of the building making possible the addition of four rooms each being 24' by 36'. A new heating and ventilating system were also added. At this time the school was also hooked up to the town water system. N.L. Wygant was awarded the contract for the addition with the exception of the heating. Reuben A Mabie was principal in 1904.

At this point there were five members of the faculty. In 1910 David D Taylor became principal and remained as principal, apparently well loved and respected, for many years.

There was much progress made during David Taylor's tenure. In the beginning students had to go to Newburgh, usually by train, if they desired a full high school education. Under Taylor's guidance in 1910 the school advanced to a Middle High School, in 1916 became a Senior Grade School and in January 1921 got the "Golden Seal" becoming a "Full High School."

The first graduates of this "Full High School" in 1921 were: Marian Barry, Earl Benjamin, Lorette Berkery and Edmund Nicklin. Both Barry and Berkery continued their educations at the New Paltz Normal School. It was during Taylor's administration that a coach and instructor of Physical Education were added to the faculty in the person of Harry Rusack.

David Taylor

By 1923 there was a faculty of eleven and a student body of about 400. The teachers in the high school at that time were David D Taylor (science and math), Mary T Holtz (English and Latin), Lucile Elwood (history and science), Viola K Burres (French and mathematics), Ina E Durland (dramatics) and Alfreda Owens (music).

George DuBois served as custodian for many years. Besides pulling the bell-rope to summon the students to class every morning, his duties included: "emptying the trash, stoking the fires, oiling the floors (to help keep down the ubiquitous chalk dust) polishing the wainscoting that girdled many of the rooms, washing the slate blackboards, and serving as truant officer into the bargain."

Another addition during Taylor's tenure was the first publication of "The Pioneer", the Marlboro High School year book. The seniors and graduates in 1923 were: Helen Berkery, Mary Ella Gaffney, Richard Gibney, Kenneth G Maybe, Louis Minard, George "Doc" Rusk (Class President) Gustav Wishoff and John Manion.

Mr. Taylor, after serving at Marlboro for nineteen years, retired in 1929 and was succeeded by Carroll F Kearney. Mr. Kearney is recognized as introducing music and art staff to the district.

The school population was growing rapidly and there was voiced the concern for a new school. In 1927 chairman of the school board, Edward C. Quimby appointed Cornelius Eckerson, Edmund S Carpenter, Rev. James F Hanley, J. Calvin Wygant, Jr., Mrs. Florence Ogden, Mrs. Patrick Manion, Mrs. Joseph Morrow and Mrs. Will (Liz) Plank a committee to present a plan for a new high school. In 1931 the high school department of the Marlborough High School had reached 91. Students from Milton and the Tuckers' Corner area of Marlborough attended high school in Highland. In 1935 the voters in the town of Marlborough voted in favor of centralization and shortly thereafter the "newer" high school (the present middle school) was built. Edward Dalby became supervising principal.

After the opening of the Marlborough Central High School, the Grand Street School was used, among other things, as a fruit exchange for a number of years. In 1975, the building gave way to "progress" and was demolished. The Marlborough Fire House now stands on the grounds of the old Grand Street School.

(Information gleaned from "Schools of the Town of Marlborough", "The Pioneer - 1923" and information courtesy of Mary DuBois)

Grand Street School Demolition 1975

Milton's "New" School

"We were thrown into the twentieth century like being shot out of a cannon!" That was Vin Russo's impression when he moved from the old Sands Avenue School to the new Milton Elementary School. The new school had indoor plumbing - no longer was it necessary to "freeze our butts off in the winter" going out to the out house. The new classrooms were not drafty like the old ones. No more old wooden floors. No more desks that had been engraved over the years with the initials of those who had occupied them. Everything was new: everything worked. The lighting system was so improved that "we had lights we could see with." But, perhaps the most exciting new feature was the new athletic field. Vin said "the most beautiful athletic field we ever could wish for".

The walk to school also was improved as now he simply had to cross the road (9W). He does emphasize that 9W of the 1930's was very different from the 9W of today. There were far fewer cars and the cars that did pass usually were driven by neighbors. One of their best sports was counting the cars that passed on 9W. Vin said it could very quickly get boring.

Vin's first teacher in the "new" school (3rd Grade) was Miss Tess Abbruzzi. Miss Abbruzzi was <u>very</u> different from his first teacher, Hattie Dickenson. "She did not strike terror in your heart". He indicated she was firm but fair and the students responded well to her. He was quite surprised to find that she was his teacher. He never knew she had been studying to be a teacher or that this was her first class. She

4

had graduated from New Paltz Normal School that summer. He had thought of her as "one of the big kids". She was the barber's daughter (Dan Abbruzzi). She was often one of the skaters on Hallock's pond. She, too, had been born and raised in Milton. Miss Abbruzzi had had Miss Hattie Dickenson as her teacher for first, second and third grade. Like Hattie Dickenson, Tess Abbruzzi was a dedicated teacher. She never married and her teaching career was very important to her.

Vin said the students realized they had to behave - "She knew us since we were born and, more important, she knew all our parents." He grinned when he said that he didn't call Miss Abbruzzi "Tess" until he was in his 50s.

Tess Abbruzzi was still living in spite of the fact that she first taught Vin almost seventy years ago. Vin opines, "It could be because she has her mother's genes and her mother lived to be 100".

Another "first year" student at the "New" Milton Elementary School was Glen Clarke who first attended Kindergarten there when the school first opened. He was just four years old and completed his elementary education (K-6) at the school.

The Sands Avenue School served the community from 1840 to 1938 - almost 100 years. The people in Milton had realized the school was outdated and a new school was needed. Mrs. Edward Young of Milton, was Grange representative on the "Committee of twenty-one". Mrs. Young was instrumental in securing the passage of a law by the state legislature in 1928 that enabled the centralization of school districts. There was Public Works Administration money for building new buildings, but the districts had to be centralized. There was a special meeting held Oct. 15, 1935 to vote on the question of centralization. Apparently it was an all day meeting in St. James Hall in Milton. The vote was for centralization by a majority of 418 in favor and 148 opposed. Elected to the new "centralized" school board were: Edgar McGowan, trustee for 5 years; Claude Hepworth, 4 years; Calvin Staples, 3 years; Edgar M Clarke, Jr., two years; and John Kramer for 1 year.

At the organizational meeting of the board, Edgar Clarke was elected President with Mrs. Will (Liz) Plank elected as clerk and Francis Kaley as treasurer. In 1935 the voters agreed to building two schools, the Marlboro School (which served as elementary school and high school as well) and the Milton School. For the first year of centralization, the old schools were used under the supervision of Edward L Dalby and much effort went into making plans for the academic program to be offered in the new school buildings.

The Dedication Program of the New Milton Grammar School was held on Wednesday evening Nov. 17, 1937. The invocation was given by the Reverend R.H.. Northrup. The Marlborough Central School Glee Club entertained the audience with several selections. The Welcome address was given by Edgar M Clarke, Jr., President of the Board of Education. Antoinette Mannese gave an address on "Our Appreciation of the New School" followed by an address by Mrs. Edward Young, Sr. The Keys to the building were presented by Gordon S. Marvel, Architect and accepted by Edgar Clarke, Jr. The audience sang "America the Beautiful" and the Benediction was given by Father Mullin. After the Dedication Program, the community was invited to inspect the new building. Milton was understandably proud of the new facility.

Thus it is the Milton Elementary School (the "new" school in the 1930s), has served the community and its students well for almost seventy years. Way to go Milton Elementary!

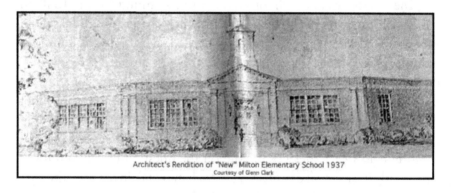

Architect's Rendition of "New" Milton Elementary School 1937
Courtesy of Glenn Clark

Ripples

"Drop a pebble in the water.- just
a splash, and it is gone,-
But there's half a hundred ripples
circling on and on and on,
Spreading, spreading from the
center, flowing on out to the sea.
And there is no way of telling
where the end is going to be.

-JAMES W. FOLEY
"Ripples"

We've all given thought to the people who dropped a pebble into our water and influenced our lives in significant ways. Vin Russo has given such thought.

"I have been reading your column in the local paper and love to read about the old days in Milton," Russo wrote in a recent letter. "My daughter, Nancy, has encouraged me to write about our family when we were kids growing up on the farm. So, I am putting together some stories to the best of my ability and memory."

Russo has wonderful memories of going to the Sands Avenue School in Milton.

A PTA pamphlet put out at the time of centralization (circa 1936) of the Marlborough Schools included this description:

"So far as it is known but one single school in the town is the original school building. Even that has had two rooms added to it. The center room of the Sands Avenue School was the original one-room school built in 1840. The school with a small hall for the boys and one for the girls contained about 150 desks. Small round chairs were used in the halls. A long platform ran the length of the school and on it the pupils stood when reciting. A large round wood stove was in the center of the school room."

Russo was born in Milton in 1930 at the homestead - still owned by the Russo family - on the corner of 9W and Milton Turnpike. "They didn't go to the hospitals to have babies in those days", Russo said. That saved the Russo's parents a lot of traveling. They had 10 children: Dom, Sam, Pat, Jeannette, Fortuna, Josephine, Anthony, Vin, Marg and Rick.

Every one of the ten had the same teacher: Hattie Dickenson. Her reputation was formidable.

"(She) drilled fear into the heart of every kid in Milton for many years," Russo said. For the Russo family, that meant 20 years before the mast of Dickenson.

"Hattie ... was typical of the old schoolmarms that taught school in this country for generations," Russo said. "Never married, her students became her children and her life. Little did we know that she took her job very seriously and that job was to teach little kids reading, writing and 'rithmatic. "

With no kindergarten, kids went directly into Miss Dickenson's class. For Russo, that was a shock. "I was the youngest kid in the whole school," he said. "I had not yet reached my fifth birthday and 'wham,' the life I knew, came to an abrupt end."

And with it, the end of childhood freedom. Or so it seemed to Russo. "With winter coming on, that meant no more skating, or skiing or sled riding," he said. "I truly thought my life was over. I thought I was condemned to a lifetime of confinement and drudge and discipline and Miss Dickenson."

Russo said there were about 10 students in each class, but each teacher had multiple classes, which meant there could be 30 students and several grades in each classroom. Karl Ernst was the principal, and also taught the upper grades. The teaching was rote repetition, and the consequences for failure to grasp the lessons were severe and immediate. "The very first lesson we had was learning the alphabet," he said. " [Miss Dickenson] did this by printing the letters on the blackboard and then we would copy them on paper. They had better be right, or else. The 'or else' was a whack on the knuckles. Believe me, you did not make many mistakes, maybe one."

After learning the printed alphabet, the students moved on to script.

Corporal "discipline" decreased as the students improved. But turn in your seat to talk to another kid, and you were sure to get a whack.

But all Russo's memories of Ms. Dickenson are not dark. Her methods, though harsh at first, were effective. "Lo and behold, as we began to catch on we felt a feeling of pride and accomplishment," he said. "I'm sure we did not know what that meant, but whatever it was, it made us feel good and, God forbid, made us feel that we wanted to go back to school and learn more."

Russo summarized the Dickenson technique: "She taught; you learned; and no nonsense."

In writing of his "first day of school," Russo captured a moment in time 75 years ago. By telling his story, he passes it on to his grandchildren, so that they may, in another 75 years, pass it on to theirs.

And the ripples go on and on and on.

Bridge to the Future

A few weeks ago I was approached by Danielle Ludwigson, a fifth grader at the Marlboro Middle School. Danielle had an assignment to interview people and get their reactions to some of the most unexpected events in the memories of the living. The assignment intrigued me, both as someone who had lived through all three of the specified events, and as an historian. I had the opportunity to speak with Mrs. Gerri

McKay, Danielle's teacher. Mrs. McKay indicated to me that Sept. 11, 2001 had caused many concerns to be expressed and felt by her young students. In an attempt to put the event in perspective, Mrs. McKay gave her students the following assignment:

As we reflect on this past year it's important to realize that what has happened to our country on September 11 is not unique to 2001. Our world and specifically our country have experienced events that have left an impression on people that they will carry forever.... Your assignment is to interview people and write down their responses to the following questions....

The first question asked was: "Where were you when you heard that Pearl Harbor was attacked?"

Fiona Barrett interviewed George Alfano. George reported that he was waiting for the bus to go to college.

Danielle Ludwigson interviewed Jacquelyn Canosa who was at her house in the Bronx,

Amber interviewed Alice Schrader who was at a basketball game and a dance when she heard the announcement.

Lou Costellano, interviewed by Joe Roberts, was in Toms River, New Jersey.

Erika Pollmann's Oma was in Germany at the time of Pearl Harbor.

Gina Nappi interviewed Madeline Porpiglia who was at Radio City Music Hall in Manhattan when Japan bombed Pearl Harbor. Joe Porpiglia was in his home when he got the news. He reported hearing the sirens blowing and realizing that service men in the area had to report back to Stewart Field.

The second question was: "What was your reaction to the news?"

Madeline Porpiglia, Gina Nappi, and Jacquelyn Canosa reported that they were young when they heard the news and didn't fully understand what was happening. George Alffano said it was a shock and Alice Schrader reported that the boy she brought to the dance later had to go into the war and was killed.

The third question was: "How had that event affected your life?"

Madeline Porpiglia told that she wrote letters to a serviceman to keep his morale up. She also indicated that food was scarce and you needed food stamps issued by the government, for example stamps for sugar. Jacquelyn Canosa also reported on the rationing of food and gas and also told how children in school started learning about wars. George Alfano had to leave college and go to war. Lou Costellano said he could never forgive the concentration camps. Erika's Oma said she became more aware when she came to the United States and hoped it would never happen again. Robin Bernard recalled how there were drives in school for the war effort, and that you couldn't buy a lot of food. Children at school had to wear tags and there were air raids and drills.

The next question was: "Where were you when you heard that President Kennedy was assassinated?"

Alice Schrader reported it was her last day working in the bank; Julia Roberts also was at work as was Mrs. Bebur. Jacquelyn Canosa was in her kitchen folding laundry - a friend called to tell her the news.

Robin Bernard was going to give birth to a daughter. Erika's grandmother was taking care of children when she heard the news as was Madeline Porpiglia. Joe Porpiglia was up in the mountains near Accord hunting. He heard the news when he went into town to get lunch. Irene Canosa was in her 7th grade class when President Kennedy was assassinated.

The next question: What were your feelings when you heard the news?"

At first Jacquelyn Canosa thought it was a joke. When she found out it was true she was very sad and went to church to pray. Irene Canosa felt horror, disbelief and surprise. Madeline Porpiglia was devastated over the assassination. She never thought something like that could happen. Joe Porpiglia felt sad and wanted to get revenge. Erika's grandmother at first thought he was going to be o.k. because the news commentators in the beginning didn't say it was serious. Then after a few hours it was reported that he had died. Mrs. Bebur felt very scared. Julia Roberts was very upset. Alice Schrader couldn't believe that anyone could be so cruel as to kill President Kennedy. Robin Bernard, who was about to give birth, had mixed emotions. She was terribly upset about the assassination, but happy that she was having a baby.

The next question: "How did that event affect your life?

Robin Bernard didn't want to spoil her daughter's birthday when everyone else was so sad. Julia Roberts was ashamed that it happened in her home state of Texas. Madeline Porpiglia couldn't believe a thing like that could happen. Alice Schrader said you learn to live with things like that and you hope the world will improve.

It isn't surprising that people have such vivid memories of where they were and what they were doing when such an event happened. What is remarkable is the specificity with which people recall their actions and reactions.

Now the questions were about the events of September 11, 2001. The first question: "Where were you when you heard that the Twin Towers and the Pentagon were attacked?"

Robin Bernard reported driving to school to drop something off. Julia Roberts was standing in her kitchen making breakfast. She was going to New York City for her birthday. Madeline Porpiglia was at home watching the news and Joe Porpiglia was dipping apples on the Porpiglia farm. Jacquelyn Canosa was also watching the news on television while the Twin Towers and the Pentagon were attacked. Andrea Canosa was in the 3rd period class in school. Erika Pollmann's grandfather was watching Fox news and saw from the time the first tower was struck. Nana Roberts reported being in school doing work when she heard the news. Andrea Carozza was at the dental office where she is employed.

The next question: "What was your reaction?"

Alice Schrader was "shocked" as was Erika Pollmann's grandfather. Jacquelyn Canosa was extremely upset that it could happen here in the United States and cried for days after. Barbara Schiavone was horrified and she also thought nothing like this could happen in the United States. Madeline Porpiglia was "sad, shocked and in fear". Joe Porpiglia was also shocked and sad and wanted revenge. Robin Bernard at first thought it was an accident. When the other buildings were hit she was very surprised. Nana Roberts was surprised that it happened in the state that has the most technology.

"How has that event affected your life this past year?" was the next question.

Nana Roberts said is showed that planes were not safe. A similar reaction was voiced by Madeline Porpiglia who indicated it makes her feel like you can't travel safely, you can't trust anyone. Erika Pollmann's grandfather said he now watches for the next event which will surely come. Irene Canosa wonders what will happen next and, as a military person, if she will get called to duty. Andrea Canosa believes that she has become more patriotic and defensive towards, not only her country, but her town. Jacquelyn Canosa said the event made her appreciate her family, and freedom, and democracy more than ever before. Andrea Carozza has come to realize you must appreciate life. Robin Bernard seconded that thought when she said "It made me want to enjoy life more, realizing how special we should treat life." Barbara Schiavone said she doesn't take anything for granted anymore. She lives "every day to the fullest."

That is the culmination of the thoughts expressed in the interviews made by the fifth grade students. It is understandable, but also quite interesting, that many of the students chose to interview their grandparents - especially with respect to Pearl Harbor. I'm sure the interviews gave the students a deeper appreciation for the events reported as well as glimpses though the eyes of others on how these events have shaped our lives. The last segment reports on the reactions of the fifth grade students themselves to the events of September 11. The question, "How would you explain September 11th to your own children...." I have tried desperately to edit the writings to cut down on the length of this report. I've failed to edit much as I've found the words so poignant that to cut some would change the intended meanings in incalculable ways. Here they are at their profoundest.

Regina Nappi -
On September 11, 2001, the World Trade Center and the Pentagon were attacked by terrorists. When I found out, I was sad. I was sad because so many people lost their lives and loved ones. Our nation was upset, but stronger than ever....

It was a very sad day and there were many more sad days to follow, but it made us all stronger as a nation. Some good things came out of 9/11. We gained stronger and better security, we all came together, and we were able to raise money to help many people whose lives were effected.....

Tyler Cary -

I would tell my kids, I was in fifth grade and during class a lot of kids were getting picked up early...Then my mom picked me up and told me the bad news. She told me that two planes hit the two World Trade Center buildings and they collapsed so thousands of people died. When I got home, I turned on the t.v.....and on almost all the channels there were people getting interviewed and they were showing the towers getting hit and falling....After that day everyone was more patriotic and had flag stickers on the cars and flags hanging from their houses.

Joseph Roberts -

I would say that it was a scary day and that your great uncle was lucky to be alive because he was supposed to be in one of the buildings, but he wasn't. I was upset because all the people around me were upset and they couldn't believe that something like this could happen to us... Some people had funerals and we helped them clean up the buildings that collapsed on 9/11. We got through every day thinking about that tragic day so we could stand tall, keep our heads held high and we are more of a country that we were before.

Ernest Borchert -

When I am older I would tell my children that on that day I was so scared to even go outside. Terrorists had highjacked four planes. They flew two planes into the Twin Towers in New York City. A third flew into the Pentagon, the command center for the United States Military. The fourth plane had crash-landed in Pennsylvania....

Nick Gattuso -

In 5th grade on 9/11/2001 in the afternoon, everyone started to go home and I was wondering why. When I got home from school my dad said, "Nick, look at the paper." It had pictures of the Twin Towers getting hit by two planes... Many people were running for their lives. When I was watching the news it showed people jumping from the burning towers. Our country has been changed by this tragedy. Now we are at war against terrorism. Airport security has been improved, there are more checks before boarding planes. There is a lot of security at public events like the World Series, Super Bowl, etc. Life in our country has been changed. We don't feel as safe anymore.

James Mazza -

About thirty years from now when my children ask for me to recall the events that took place of September 11th I'd say a few things. I would tell them of the bravery and courage shown on that day. 3,000 people died at the World Trade Center and more than 800 people died in the Pentagon. There was also an additional 200 that died in a plane flying over Pennsylvania.... At the time of the tragedy I was minding my own business doing the morning routine; getting my stuff out for my fifth grade class. It was a normal day for me. No one in school said anything. In fact I really didn't know any details until I got home.... In the year that followed the nation mourned for those who died. The security of airports and other highly important locations increased significantly. The terrorists meant to pull us apart but they just made us stand together.... Later on I learned one of my mother's friend's brother was a New York Firefighter. He died in one of the towers. When the DNA tests were done they learned somebody else's DNA was mixed in with his. The most logical answer is that a boy was under his coat. He was rushing the boy out of the building. The fireman died.... After a while a few things got back to normal, but some things will never be the same.

Caitlyn Russ -

I would tell my kids that on September 11th I was in the car on the way to school. When, all of a sudden, I heard something terrible on the radio. I heard that planes hit both of the Twin Towers. I also heard that a plane hit the Pentagon.... My feelings about 9/11 were weird because I had never felt that way in my whole life. I was really upset. Those poor, innocent people lost their lives. I felt like someone tore a piece of my heart out.

I don't want to run the risk of patronizing the students, as I consider them young in years, not in maturity. Who was it said, "Out of the mouths of babes..."? As indicated previously, many of the students interviewed their grandparents. In the above they are considering what they might tell their children. While I think they naturally would have difficulty envisioning it, they could tell the same stories to their grandchildren. If they were to tell their grandchildren also of the stories told them by their grandparents, what a rich history they would be passing on. If so, from 1945 - the date of the bombing of Pearl Harbor - as told to them by their grandparents - to the date when they would be telling their grandchildren would be approximately 100 years. This is the stuff of which vibrant history is made.

I have asked Mrs. McKay to permit me to incorporate some of the above into the town archives. I think in 100 years or so, there would be interest in reading this material.

Many thanks to Mrs. McKay and her students - a well conceived assignment that was very well executed.

NorthWest Territory

Gerhard Brunfeindt
at the three corners

Look at a map of the town of Marlborough and notice how in the northwest corner it comes to a pretty sharp angle. Ever wonder just where that corner actually lies? The kids in that area go to the Highland schools and the grown up folks tend to do their shopping and socializing in places other than Marlborough. I had the opportunity recently to explore just where that NW corner of town really is. My host was Gerhard Burfeindt who was raised in the area. Gerhard was able to stand in the exact spot where the towns of Marlborough, Plattekill and Lloyd meet. He offered the information that at one time there was a fence from that spot along the Lloyd border.

Gerhard remembers going to the TriBorough School - which sits in Plattekill on the Marlborough border just south of the Lloyd town line. The school was a two room school house that provided educational opportunities for roughly twenty students from Plattekill, Marlborough and Lloyd.

Gerhard remembers the school as two rooms. The first for grades 1-4 and the second for grades 5-8. Each year, as you moved up a grade, you moved over one row. His teacher for 1-4 was Mrs. Powers. For grades 5-8 he had Rose Capozzi. Mr. Sylvio Chaissan was the superintendent then Willard Rhoades. It was in 1935 that the school was moved and added to.

Gerhard was also able to show me the original sign that hung on the TriBorough School. Though difficult to read, it says -
"School District
#9 Plattekill
#8 Marlboro
#6 Lloyd"

That area, is known as Sugar Hollow or Pancake Hollow and had the reputation of having seven mills within seven miles. Pancake Hollow has long been the bailiwick of the Browns and the Palmateers. One source indicates the Peter Palmateer's father, John, first came to the area from Kingston which he left after the burning in Kingston in 1777. Peter Palmateer was one of the Palmateers from the area who was in the Revolutionary War. I find Palmateers in New York since 1683 (List of Inhabitants of Colonial New York (Edmund Bailey O'Callaghan excerpted by Rosanne Conway - p 114)). Peter was born June 14, 1766 and died Sept. 20, 1849 (Ulster County in the Revolution - edited by Ruth P Heidgerd, 1977). If so, he was quite young when he gave service to the rebelling colonies. There are a number of inhabitants of Pancake Hollow who carry the name Palmateer to this day - I suspect progeny of Peter and his descendants.

Peter's wife, Elizabeth Johnson Palmateer, made a will Feb. 8, 1851 and in the will mentions , "I give and bequeath to ... my daughter, Eliza, wife of Joseph Brown,...". Thus the Brown connection.

I'd like to thank my research cohorts for the day, Gerhard Burfiendt, Dotty Gruner (Town of Plattekill Historian) and Jeffrey Burfiendt.

1919 Graduation

Twenty five years ago - From Record of June 24, 1914

The first annual commencement exercises of the Marlborough High School were held in Memorial Hall on Monday evening. The grammar school graduated a large class, but there were only three who attained the distinction of being the first graduates from the Marlborough High School. Grave and dignified indeed, as became the president of the class was Calvin Wygant and dainty and charming looked the two young ladies - Agnes Clancey and Helen Banker - who shared honors with him. The girls intend to enter Normal school when they reach the required ages.

(Marl. Record - June 30, 1939)

Memorial Hall

50th Reunion

**"Those were the days, my friend...
We thought they'd never end..."**

It was only yesterday, wasn't it when our stomachs were all atwitter at the thought of us marching down the center aisle in the gym to the tune of "Pomp and Circumstance"? We'd been through all the rites of passage in high school -

Junior Prom entitled, "Deep In The Blue" was held in the profusely decorated gym of the high school (the present middle school). A good part of the fun of planning and holding the Junior Prom was getting together to do the decorations;

Athletics: Football, Cross Country, Track, and Basketball (boys and girls) along with the affiliated Cheerleaders and Athletic Association;

Music: Girls' Chorus, Mixed Chorus, Senior Band and Junior Band;

Service groups: the Police Force, the Fire Squad and Monitor Squad, the Amplifier Squad, Camera Club, Leaders Club, the Re-Echo, the Broadcasting Club, and the Library Club;

Senior Play: "The Great Scotts" directed by Mr. Kirby, was performed to a full house;

Specialty groups: Yearbook Staff, Debate Club, Future Farmers, 4-H Club, Marlboro Spark Plugs;

Various semi political offices that were so crucial in developing our civic attitudes and skills: Mid-Hudson Student Congress, Student Council and, especially, Senior Class Officers with President, Vinnie Vasile, Vice President, Betsy Hutchins, Secretary, Joyce Krauss and Treasurer, James Manion.

Were our stomachs atwitter again? Who would be there? Who would we remember? Who would remember us? As we stepped through the doors at the Ships Lantern Inn, our fears melted away with the last fifty years. There were the same people with whom we had shared lunches, gossip, pajama parties, teen-age crushes. Voices rose in excitement as handshakes, hugs and kisses were exchanged. Friends whipped out pictures - pictures of fifty years ago as well as recent pictures of children and grandchildren. Yes, there were visible physical changes - hair had thinned and grayed, eyes needed glasses, frames were more rotund. Were those our own teeth? Yet, as much as people changed, that much they also remained the same. The faces of fifty years ago emerged through the smiling faces that were now before us.

Perhaps even more remarkable, we were so pleased to recognize the human traits, the spirits, the souls that had endeared these classmates to us so long ago, still dwelt in those more aged, wizened frames. Still evident were the gleams in the eyes, the turned up lips, the tilts of the heads that warned us of a joke. When our eyes met, we recognized the sincerity behind the actions. When there was pain, it was lessened by a knowing arm around the shoulder.

During dinner, the conversations moved quickly with a lot of , "Do you remember...?". We discussed: Edmund Alvut, who had been our principal, Paul Georgini, Veronica Ronkese, Clarence Spitzer and Mr. Cordier - teachers who we had thought were tough old birds..... we thanked them, belatedly, for caring enough to expect the best from us. We remembered the good reputation that the class of '53 had had. The teachers had all liked us. We were considered a very close, cohesive class. We were admired by classes both before and after us.

Perhaps the most memorable part of the evening was the recognition of how lucky we all had been growing up and going to school in a community like Marlborough. We felt we had had very innocent,, wholesome, yet very rich early years thanks to a supportive school and community. Is it too late after 50 years to say, "Thank you"?

Standing - Mike Rodelli, George Rusk, Dennie O'Connor, Shirley (Patterson) Koran, Joe Casscles, Sabra (McElrath) Jesionek, Carol Ann (Casscles) Purtell, Carole

(Mondello) Bushnell, June (Atkins) Kohl, Irene (Schlesinger) Stevens, Joan (Affuso) Fazio, Oliver Mackey, Andrew Wienert

Middle Row - Frances (Fabiano) Dickinson, Margie (Williams) Peplow, Camille Affuso, Joyce (Krauss) Morris, Chris (Collins) Noeltner, Valeria (Dawes) Terwilliger, Cynthia (Carpenter) Gervais, Carol (Strong) Hayes, Bob Nicklin, MaryLou (Hennekens) Mahan

Sitting in front - Jimmy Manion, Richard Mazzella

Recently the Marlboro graduating class of 1953 held its 50th Reunion with a dinner at the Ships' Lantern Inn in Milton. The motivating force behind the reunion was Camille Affuso. Various awards were made including: traveling the greatest distance - Dennis O'Connor and most children - George Rusk. Joseph Casscles led in a moment of prayer for those classmates who have crossed over - Mary DeSantis, Mary Dirago, Walter Richards, Vincent Vasile and Elizabeth Shurter.

Unable to attend were: James Atkins, Sharlene (Barry) Primivera, Ed Crosby, Nancy (Fellicello) Roberts, Jack Ferguson, Jean (Greiner) Betters, Marianne (Hampel) Lines, Betsy (Hutchins) Wilklow, Bob Linsig, Patricia (Quinn) Fellicello, Kathleen (Vasile) Amaro, Nancy (Weinert) Tomitz and Charles Wilson.

Of Things Spiritual

Amity Baptist Church, wooden church in the Gothic style, 310 West 54th Street, N.Y.C. Photograph. 1885

The Gift that Keeps on Giving

It was 100 years ago that a railroad train chugged into the West Shore station burdened with a complete building. The building was Amity Chapel, shipped from 54th Street in New York City to find a new setting on a hillside in Marlboro. The chapel had a rich history before arriving in Marlborough. The first pastor of Amity Baptist Church in 1832 was the Reverend William R Williams. He was, reputedly, an attorney who became a minister. He served in that position from 1832 until 1885 when his son, (also an attorney turned minister) Leighton Williams, succeeded him.

WILLIAM R. WILLIAMS, D. D., LL. D.,
First Pastor of Amity Baptist Church.
1832-1885.

At that point the Williamses were already known to Marlborough. In 1864, the first deed I find into Williams, 26 acres were sold by Thomas Bingham to Mary Williams (mother of Leighton) and another. In 1865 another 7 acres were added. In 1876 the Taylors sold 9A to Williams. In 1884 they added to the main house on their property. There was a big porch around the house with an upper and lower deck. The last purchase was in 1911 from Sleight and contained almost 30 acres. All told the Williamses at one time owned over 70 acres in Marlborough - the lands included (all between the Orange County line and Bingham Road) the Truncali farm, the Wilklow's land and Amity Chapel land as well as more.

Rev. Leighton Williams
courtesy of Betsy Wilklow

Leighton Williams was the pastor of Amity Baptist Church from 1885. The church, on 54th Street in New York City launched a new building project. The old chapel was destined to be destroyed when Mary Williams decided it should be moved to her land in Marlboro. It is believed that she paid for the shipping to Marlborough. The building was taken apart section by section and hauled on flat cars to the Marlborough station. There it was met by large flat wagons and a few sledges drawn by horses. The wagons and sledges were driven by local folk which included some Cosmans, some Binghams and others.

Addison Wilklow, Jr.

In an interview with Addison, Bill and Betsy Wilklow, they indicated the foundation had been dug by hand by a father and son, but could not recall the names. Local townspeople held an old fashioned building "bee" and the building was reassembled on its present location.

William Wilklow

In 1907 Addison Wilklow, Sr. was born. Shortly thereafter his parents died leaving him an orphan. He found himself in an orphanage on Montgomery Street in Newburgh. Leighton Williams and his wife, Nellie Grant Winterton, adopted Addison and brought him into their home. Leighton had been a successful lawyer with Andrew Greene's firm - one of the most prominent in New York City. His brother, Mornay, was also an attorney. Nellie was considered to be quite a beauty and is believed to have been a niece to General (and President) U.S. Grant. Her father is thought to have been an insurance adjuster for the Chicago fire of 1871, and one sister, Mary Grace Quackenboro is thought to have been a Special Attorney for the Justice Department investigating the mistreatment of Italian immigrants. Another sister, Jesse Arnold Day, married wealth and became a benefactor of the church. The church was also very involved in the Fresh Air Fund and many youngsters from New York City were given refuge from the heat of the city. Indeed Leighton Williams is credited with being one of the prime movers for the Fresh Air Fund. For decades there were summer "pilgrimages" to Amity Chapel from the city church. Cottages were built for summer occupancy. Religious meetings were held there.

In a pamphlet advertising the fifteenth annual Conference of "The Brotherhood of the Kingdom" to be held in Marlborough-on-Hudson August 2-6, 1909 it states: "A reception and devotional meeting will be held at the residence of Dr. and Mrs. Leighton Williams, on Monday evening, August 2, at eight o'clock." It goes on to say Marlborough is "in the midst of vine-clad hills and charming scenery." The conference was to be held on a hilltop 500 feet above the river "with a panoramic view in all directions." Arrangements were to be made for accommodations in cottages and in tents for the conference attendees. Meals were slated to cost $1 per day.

In 1910 Dr. and Mrs. Williams presented Amity Chapel with a modern organ. There were two additions put on the building - one for a pipe organ and another to house the rather extensive library of Leighton Williams.

Leighton Williams for long periods of time filled in as pastor for the Lattingtown Baptist Church until they were able to engage a full time minister. Williams later went, first to New Paltz, and then to Kingston where he was rector of St. John's Episcopal church from 1918 to 1921. Dr. Williams then served Christ Episcopal Church in Marlboro from 1921 to 1932. Indeed, Addison Wilklow, Jr. was born in the Episcopal Rectory in 1931. By 1934 when Bill Wilklow was born, the Williamses were living in the big house on their Bingham Street property.

Leighton Williams died in 1935 and his wife in 1938. The church was inactive for a period of time, but then revived, in part by the Reverend Moncada, to once again serve the Marlborough community. The church is presently known as the Chapel Hill Bible Church. The congregation is very proud that the church has been informed that the chapel will be listed on the National Register. Thanks for their efforts need to go to George Graziosi, Mike Hannigan and Jennifer VanBuren. The present minister is the Reverend Ray Spangler.

A Centennial Celebration is being planned for this fall and a book relating the history of the chapel is in the works.

Thus it is that the gift from Leighton Williams, lo those many years ago, still thrives and is a source of inspiration, now, and hopefully for many years in the future.

The Famous and Infamous
Another of History's Mysteries

Our sleuth today is Tim Small, a delightful young man from Nebraska, working on a graduate thesis. He has done extensive work in the area of Art History with an emphasis on Winslow Homer. Small is in the process of trying to find proof that Marlborough's own Mary Hallock Foote was one of the models that Winslow Homer used in his works. Small provided us with a photograph of Mary Hallock Foote taken in 1875. which he is comparing with a watercolor done by Winslow Homer in 1875 ......

Mary Hallock Foote photograph 1875

Girl at the Window - Winslow Homer 1875
New Britain Museum of Art

A key element of Small's theory that Foote was one of Homer's models is her friendship with Helena de Kay Gilder. That friendship began during their student days at Cooper Union in New York City in the mid-1860s and lasted for several decades. Helena married Richard Watson Gilder, editor of "Century Magazine." Gilder encouraged Foote's writing and helped get her stories published in some of the better-known publications of the time. Helena is known to have modeled for Homer. Small believes it is likely that Homer and Foote knew each other, and that Homer could have mentored Foote's writing and illustrating career.

Mary Hallock Foote Birthplace
9W Milton

Foote was born in Milton in 1847. She was the daughter of Nathaniel and Ann Burling Hallock, who are buried at the Hallock cemetery in Milton near the Town Park. It is believed that Nathaniel built his house around 1830. The house at one time was the pride of the neighborhood.

The Nathaniel Hallock House is a 16 room frame building with four original fireplaces, 14 foot ceilings on the first floor and 12 foot ceilings on the second floor. It also has the original 12 inch floor boards and the original ceiling beams in the Tap Room. The hinges and doorknobs are also original.

Some off the window panes are original and the wall construction is brick-lined with plaster. The house was built in sections. Before the new highway was put through there was a gravity flow of water into the house and in fountains outdoors. The tulip trees on the premises measure five feet in diameter.

Mar Hallock Foote was born in the original part of the house. (Information from the Marlborough House Survey of 1967)

Mary Hallock Foote wrote her memoirs in a book entitled, "A Victorian Gentlewoman in the Far West." The book is available at the Sarah Hull Hallock Library in Milton. Sarah Hull Hallock was aunt to Mary Hallock Foote.

Music to My Ears

We have long been blessed with the sounds of music in Marlborough. Nature has provided us with the soft tinkle of water running over stones in a brook; the soft drumbeat of a Spring rain, the loud bass drum sound of distant thunder. When man first produced music is lost in the distant mist of history, but it doesn't take much to conjure up the picture of a young Native American playing his handmade flute while sitting on the banks of Old Man's Creek.

Nothing is noted about the music heard by the first Europeans to inhabit our town. Did Lewis DuBois provide any type of music at social gatherings at his home which is dated c 1757? Did Anning Smith march to the sound of flute and drum when he left Marlborough to attend to the Revolutionary War?

We can suppose that music has long played a part in local church services. In 1859, under the pastorate of Rev. S. H. Jagger, the Presbyterian Church installed a bell in the first church building which stood on Main Street (9W).

Perhaps Marlborough's best loved musician was George A Badner. "George A Badner is son of John Badner, and leader of the Marlborough Cornet Band, and also plays in Lent & Badner's orchestra (Cochrane, 1887, p 194).

George A Badner was also a member of Knights of Pythias, established 1883, and the Advance Lodge of Odd Fellows, established 1882. The Advance Lodge Band often provided music to an appreciative audience and were on tap for many of the community celebrations.

In 1996 photo "Deet Badner" shows, with pride, the Badner cornet.

"Deet" Badner with Badner cornet - 1996

I've been unable to ascertain exactly when the first Marlborough High School band was organized.

From Record of June 24, 1914

"The first annual commencement exercises of the Marlborough High School were held in Memorial Hall on Monday evening...There were only three who attained the distinction of being the first graduates from the Marlborough High School. Since there were only 3 graduating, it is assumed they didn't have the school population to support a band.

However, by 1946 the band was in full swing and a very popular activity.

Back Row - Frank Jarmino (?), Edward Smith, Vito Valentino, Edmond Shortt, John Corrado, Barton Harris
Middle Row - Faith Sears, Howard Quimby, Latson Andrews, Kathleen Kent, Carol Wygant, Dominick LoFaro, Phyllis Palmer, Leonard Sarinski, (?)
Front Row - Sally Clarke, Bill Stant, Panthea Kaplin, Tessi Redelli, Doris Dalby, Doris Polizzi, Catherine Mackey, Mary Grace Ferrara, Alfred Shortt
Sitting - Charlie Clancy, Josie Cutrone, Joe Masay(?)

The best musicians in the Class of 1953 were: Valeria Dawes, cornet; Eddie Crosby, drums; Joe Casscles, tuba; Vinnie Vasile, cornet; Jimmy Manion, trombone; Chris Collins, clarinet; Bob Nicklin, alto sax; Jeannie Griener, horn; Bob Linsig, bell lyre; Sabra McElrath, trombone and Margie Williams, cymbals - and, who can forget Jack Ferguson on the sax playing "In the Mood". I tinkered with cymbals, bell lyre and oboe - had the interest but not the talent. Ten of the forty-one graduating seniors were members of senior band that year.

In the recent past Wendell Bloomer had for many years lent his tenor voice to the Presbyterian choir as Rose Dugan sang the high notes at the Catholic services. Margaret Faurie over a tenure of many years delighted the Lattingtown Baptist Church with fine music played on the old pump organ at that church.

This tradition of fine music is kept alive today by Tony Falco with his many concerts at both his home and the Cluett Schantz Memorial Park.

Making Connections

I had the pleasure of knowing Lillian Webber who was a prime player in the Open Classroom movement in education in the 1960s. Lillian claimed that all of education was making connections - connections between things we know and things we've just learned, connections between past and present, connections between things we know but never realized were connected.

A while ago, the 53ers were meeting for lunch at the Raccoon. Carol Ann Casscles Purtell brought a book she thought I would be interested in reading, "In the Early Morning" written by Marion Edey. As Carol Ann suggested, the book was delightful. Written from the perspective of a 10 year old girl growing up at Danskammer the story is chock full of the sights, sounds, smells and tastes of Danskammer in the late 1800s.

Marion writes only a little of her family, but one senses the deep affection she had for the David Maitland Armstrong family that was her own. David Maitland was the grandson of Colonel William Armstrong who had come to America with the British Army during the Revolution and stayed on. The Armstrongs' home was known as "Danskammer". Marion's mother was descended from Peter Stuyvesant.

"Danskammer was neither a convenient nor a beautiful house, too haphazard and unplanned-looking - as indeed it had a right to be, with one end two hundred years old and small, comparatively new wing at the other. But though shabby in its tangle of Virginia creeper and Dutchman's pipe it had settled so comfortably into the level lawn among the trees that the general impression was pleasant and homelike."

Marion writes little about the art that was such an important factor in her family. Her father, D. Maitland, became a well known artist and was a friend of George Innes. He was especially skilled and talented in the area of stained glass windows. At that time he was recognized as being in the same league with La Farge, who was also a friend, and Tiffany. His windows are still to be found in some of the most prestigious churches in the U.S.

"The stepladder usually stood by a large charcoal cartoon thumb-tacked to the bare wall, and there was often the glass head of a saint or a cherub affixed to the north window; part of the "flesh", as it was rather unpleasantly known in the stained-glass world, in due time to be incorporated in one of the church windows designed by Papa."

D. Maitland trained two of his daughters in the field also. His daughter, Helen, became especially well known for her work in stained glass faces and material folds.

"A Lay figure named Maude (a dummy) lurked in a corner. Although her face had partly disintegrated the jointed limbs could take and keep any position. Maude had posed under a variety of draperies for pretty nearly everyone from Abraham to Dorcas."

Helen Maitland Armstrong created several of the windows in Christ Episcopal Church in Marlboro. She was to become her father's partner in the field and they both worked on at least one of the church windows.

D. Maitland's brother, William Henry, purchased the property of the Gomez Mill House and lived there from 1862 to 1904. At the Gomez Mill House is a painting by D. Maitland Armstrong of his son, Edward, in front of the fireplace at Danskammer.

A few particularly interesting parts of the book were as follows:

Cutting ice - First she talks of the "ice marker" - something like a mowing machine with two enormous knives underneath. The marker dug long lines as it moved across the ice - marking it off into strips. After the ice was marked two men would saw through the ice with their double ice saw - "scrape-scrape, scrape-scrape, like rusty music". Then the me
a pole with a spike on it along the channel to
was hauling the ice out of the water and load

Their education - the children on fou
Rector of the Episcopal Church for sch
arithmetic.

Lime Kilns - "On the shore were two
for burning the limestone which cropp
their well water so hard.

The Light House at the Point - She
Government Boat would steam up the r
the big light and coal for the lightkeeper

After reading the book, I was intereste
dows in Christ Church. I called the Rever
visit from me and my camera. I was able t
of the windows and was particularly impres
We were both pleased to find the window
Maitland and Helen Maitland Armstrong.
Hawksley, who had been Rector of the chu

The Reverend Brooks
and the Marion Edey stone

We then headed to the cemetery. Can you imagine how pleased I was to find the gravestone of Marion Armstrong Edey? I told the good Reverend that after having read her book, I felt a special affinity for her.

So here we have the connections - Lillian Webber; Carol Ann Purtell and the 53ers; Marion Armstrong and her book; cutting ice; Colonel William Armstrong; Peter Stuyvesant; D. Maitland Armstrong and his daughter, Helen; George Innes; Danskammer; Gomez Mill House; Christ Church Marlboro; and the Reverend Samuel Hawksley.

Isn't History wonderful?

Writer's note - After finishing the book, I checked the web and was able to pick up my own copy for less than $5 + shipping - if interested, check it out.

Also - I got a nice e/mail from Paul Georgini, once Superintendent of Schools in Marlborough, regarding a previous article. He reports that he too owns the Hudson!

A President in the Making (1)

He came from "good" stock. The first forebear to touch American soil was Edward who arrived from England in 1692. Edward had a son, Edward, who had a son, John. John was the Saratoga County Court Judge from 1809 to 1818. John had at least two

John W Taylor was a member of indeed Speaker of the House from to 1827, Both terms immediately reported that his ringing speech agair Compromise is quoted in Horace Gr

Richard, was born in 1777 anc Onondaga County, NY. He was m Phebe Clark who bore him two so Both Richard and Phebe had child family home was indeed a busy one

Elisha E.L. was educated at Madison University, in Hamilton, NY (1831-1839) and after a year more of graduate work was prepared for ministerial services.

Elisha E.L. Taylor

35

During his college years at Hamilton Elisha met a young boarding-school girl, "The prettiest girl in the school," Mary Jane Perkins, second daughter of the Reverend Aaron Perkins.

The Reverend Perkins was the first full time Minister at the Baptist Church of Lattingtown. He was called to the pulpit in 1812. He is remembered in history as one of their most beloved preachers. Cochrane (The History of the Town of Marlborough, 1887 by Charles H Cochrane) reports:

"There are old people now (1887) living in the vicinity whose eyes glisten with delight as they speak of the days and years when Elder Perkins preached in Lattintown, when the meeting-house, with its capacious gallery, proved too small to accommodate the congregation, and those who arrived latest drove up to the sides and ends of the meeting-house and sat in their wagons...and listened, and loved to listen, to the preached word."

Mary Jane's mother was Deborah Smith, granddaughter to Anning Smith.

The Reverend Elisha Taylor served many years at the Pierrepont Street Baptist Church in Brooklyn as well as being involved in the Home Mission Society with special charge of schools for the American Indians. Elisha E. L. and Mary Jane (Perkins) Taylor were the parents of six sons and three daughters. James Monroe Taylor was born in 184 there were economic constraints due a minister's salary, each of the childrer

The boys were prepared for college at a boarding school called "The Essex Seminary" in Essex, Connecticut. James was sent to Essex in 1859 when only eleven years of age. The school was under the auspices of a Mr. Cummings and had about twenty boys enrolled. Cummings himself taught all the classes. He must have been an interesting personality as

James Monroe Taylor

36

he bought a sail boat and brought the whole school sailing while at the same time holding classes in Grammar and public speaking.

One of the essays written by James Monroe Taylor while attending Essex was a report on a trip to New York City. He reported that in 1858 he was taken to New York City to witness the celebration of the laying of the Atlantic Cable. Cyrus Field, the man responsible for laying the telegraph rode through the streets of New York bowing to the crowds assembled.

Interesting to note - about thirty years later the Taylors dined with Cyrus Field. Field told them when at last the cables were joined and tested showing that messages passed, he went down into his room and wept.

In 1863, when James Monroe was sixteen years of age, his father, Doctor Elisha Taylor, threatened by poor health, purchased a home in Marlborough from Thomas Bingham. There was a large house with twenty acres of land - later more acreage was added and it amounted to 100 acres. Here, from just before James entered University, for ten years this home became the center of family life. (This is presently the Truncali house and farm). Mary Jane (Perkins) Taylor had been born in Marlborough, so this was indeed a welcome homecoming. The road to 9W from the Taylor's house was once known as Taylor Road.

The house stood high on a hill with a magnificent view of the Hudson River and the surrounding hills and mountains. There was a row of tall, lush maple trees lining the drive to the house. Surrounding the house on three sides was a porch where one could sit and admire the view. The house had many windows and two living-rooms which extended straight through the house and ended in French windows on the porch. There was a long dining-room with a bay window again glimpsing the river.

It was a working farm and thus included berry patches, a vineyard and hay-meadows. James, just sixteen years old at the time, was put in charge of managing the farm during the frequent absences of his father. James was reading Walter Scott's poems that summer and one of his siblings reported that when picking got boring, James would start calling out couplets of Marmion which the others then carried on one by one. The sibling later said, "This robust poem is indelibly associated for all of us with the Marlboro berry patch".

What did the Taylor offspring do to pass their time in Marlborough?

Apparently driving horses was high on the list. The father, Elisha, had a soft spot for spirited horses and taught his children to ride and drive. The Taylors must have had a carriage house as one deed from 1866 mentions a right of way leading from the highway to the barn along the E side of the carriage house granted to EEL Taylor by Thomas Bingham. They also fished, caught frogs, found bird nests - even a hawk nest once - played "one old cat," "fungoes," pitched Quoits and played croquet. as well as enjoyed the many weekend visitors. It's been reported that as many as twenty-four family and friends would sit down at the table.

More to come.........................

A President in the Making (2)

James Monroe Taylor entered the University of Rochester in 1864 at the age of sixteen and graduated in 1868. During this time the house was enlarged by another story. One of the new rooms was always referred to as "Jim's room." In a letter to a friend in 1866 James Monroe writes about being very busy with the hay and harvesting and thus has had little time to read and study. In another letter in 1867 he writes to his friend about a planned twenty-five mile drive to Cornwall and Canterbury. In 1866 he tells his friend, "I am at present enjoying the fullest ease. I ride a great deal, and am _____ ."

In 1871 he spent a year of study abroad. In 1872 he wrote to Kate Huntington, who would become his bride, "I must go to Marlboro, and if you could know just how I feel, so anxious to get into the country again, away from everyone but our own family...I want to be in Marlboro more than in any place under the sun...but to enjoy it thoroughly, I need you." Interestingly it was addressed to "Miss Huntington".

His father, Elisha E. L. Taylor

James Monroe Taylor at Graduation from the University of Rochester, 1868.

died. It was a difficult time for James Monroe. The young man of twenty-one recuperated from his loss at Marlborough. In a letter to a friend he remarks, "What have I done? Roasted, trimmed vines, driven horses, loafed!". In 1872 his mother passed away with him at her bedside.

In 1882 we find that James Monroe Taylor, his mother and father both deceased, divests himself of the last piece of property and the Taylor home in Marlboro.

He earned D.D. degrees from Rochester Theological Seminary in 1886 and Yale University in 1901 as well as an LL.D. from Rutgers. He served as a minister for several years and in 1886 received the call to become the president of Vassar College. His accomplishments at Vassar were extraordinary.

Vassar was founded by Matthew Vassar in 1861 and opened in 1865. In 1886 Vassar had five buildings and the number of students had fallen to 291 - 50 of whom were in the preparatory department.

In 1887 Charles Dickens was invited to read from his works.

In 1888 Dr. Taylor reported that graduate courses were being offered.

In 1889 Vassar was represented at the Exposition Universelle at Paris by an exhibition of photographs, building plans and curricula of study.

In 1889 the Department of Physical Education was the first regularly organized department of its kind in an American college.

In 1889 the May Day customs with a Maypole were revived.

He instituted a program whereby small groups of seniors were given the privilege of dining with the President and Mrs. Taylor - thus he was able to insure real acquaintance with his students.

On Thanksgiving Day the President and his wife were at home to the whole college.

During the period, 1886-1895 new buildings were added; the Conservatory, the Gymnasium, the first new residence hall and Strong.

The preparatory department had been abolished.

The number of students increased from 291 to 538.

As long as he remained at Vassar, Doctor Taylor was not only President, but Professor, teaching ethics.

In 1899 he was summoned to take the position of President of Brown University. The students, the faculty and the alumnae were jubilant when he refused that honor.

In his later years at Vassar, his time was invested heavily in obtaining endowments to further strengthen its program. In 1903 he announced that John D Rockerfeller had promised to contribute dollar for dollar up to $200,000 for all that the College could raise.

Another interesting tidbit comes to our attention. In 1907 Vassar President Dr. James Monroe Taylor had forbid Suffrage meetings on campus. Inez Mulholland, Vassar class of 1909 was to become a central figure in grassroots organizing for Women's Suffrage. She held unofficial and somewhat clandestine "classes" at Vassar. On March 13, 1913 she led the Suffrage march in Washington in which over 1000 women actively participated. Inez was the moving force and organizer of student demonstrations and petitions at Vassar. In 1914 President Taylor succumbed to pressure and granted permission for a "women's Suffrage club" to exist officially on campus.

In 1912 Dr. Taylor made a nostalgic trip to his "home" town and gave an address at Old Home Week in Marlborough. Plank reports, "Perhaps the greatest event ever held in the town was Old Home Week celebrated in the fall of 1912. Governor Alfred E Smith and Judge Alton B Parker, one time Democratic candidate for president, were guests of honor, as well as...other prominent individuals" (History of Marlborough, Will Plank, pg 13).

In 1914 Dr. Taylor resigned his position with Vassar amid numerous voicings of thanks and well wishes. After chapel on his last night at Vassar, the students, dressed in white formed two lines between which the Taylors could exit and "bravely tried to sing their farewell song." In 1915 Taylor Hall at Vassar was dedicated to James Monroe Taylor.

In 1915 Taylor collaborated with Elizabeth Hazelton Haight to write "Vassar", a history of the College. Taylor had served as President of Vassar College from 1886 to 1914 - a total of 28 years.

James Monroe Taylor died in 1916 dearly loved by the Vassar Community and well respected in academia the world over. He did us proud!

(Please note - much of the information in the above has been gleaned from "The Life & Letters of James Monroe Taylor", written by Elizabeth Hazelton Haight, Professor of Latin at Vassar, 1919. It has not been ascertained whether or not Elizabeth was related to the Marlborough Haights.)

The Adopted Son

Milton on the Hudson has for over a century proudly embraced, as an adopted son, George Inness, the famous American landscape painter. Inness spent many of his most productive summers in Milton painting some of his most cherished works. He gloried in the hills and dales that surrounded the then sleepy lit-tle hamlet, so close to the beautiful "American Rhine", peaceful, bucolic and so nearly the "forest primeval". "The title "father of the American landscape" fits him better than it does anyone else. But he preferred what he called 'civilized landscape' - places which suggest the nearness of man as a farmer and builder - to the entirely untamed wilderness." (Alfred Werner, Inness Landscapes, Watson-Guptill Pub., NY, 1973)

LeRoy Ireland (The Works of George Inness, University of Texas Press) credits Inness with over 1,500 paintings. Twenty one of Inness's paintings are entitled either "Milton" or "Milton on the Hudson" (there are also eight entitled simply, "Moonlight", five "Moonrise" and eight "Morning"). There are a good number of others that have Milton in the title or, were painted in Milton with titles denoting such things as "Mill", "Pond" or "Orchard".

There have been several texts that report that Inness stayed at the home of Asia Hallock. Glenn Clarke and I have spent the last few years trying to determine just who Asia Hallock was. Glenn had lent me a book (Oil Paintings & Water-colors by George Inness, American Art Assoc., NYC, 1927) that stated, "Several of the Inness landscapes were painted by him at Milton-on-the-Hudson on the farm of the hospitable Quakeress, Mrs. Asia Hallock, at whose house the family passed many delightful summers." Who was this Mrs. Asia Hallock?

In <u>Our Quaker Forbears</u> edited by Theodora M Carrell (in the Milton Library) it states:

In a gabled house overlooking the river, surrounded by trees through which the placid Hudson was seen, lived Aunt Sarah Hallock, worker for the suffrage for women, and her sister Cousin Dorcas Hull...My diary speaks of the lovely views of the river and of guests in the house, Mrs. Inness, wife of George Inness, the landscape painter, who was shut in his room that day because of illness.

AHA! Where the name Asia came from is still a mystery. Sarah was married to Edward Hallock (born c 1796 - died c 1859). In 1861 Nathaniel Hallock (brother to Sarah's husband, Edward) sold to Sarah Hallock and Dorcus Hull four acres and 18 perches of land along the Post Road (old 9W going through the center of Milton) and East along the road that leads from the Post Road to the river (Old Indian Road). Dorcus Hull was sister to Sarah Hull Hallock. Sarah Hull Hallock was the original benefactor of the Milton Library which still bears her name. Their home became a notable boarding house of that time.

The next question that plagues one is, "What first brought George Inness to Milton?" He was born near Newburgh in 1825. I believe it was to the West of Newburgh. But, his family moved from the area while he was a small child.

In a previous article in the Southern Ulster Times, I reported on David Maitland Armstrong, the renowned stain glass artist. Armstrong and Inness were both in Rome, Italy in the 1860's and formed a friendship there. Armstrong came from just below the Ulster/Orange County borders and thus was

connection.

The Hallocks were noted
Hull Hallock was involved
Note that Carrell (op. cit.) d
for women...Her face, too, v
charming, gifted and well kn
Sarah Hull Hallock,, Susan I
Hull, lamenting the death o
been at one of the early Won
mentions having been to Sar

It has been noted that,

On the Farm, Milton, NY

Here a nursemaid wheels a baby in a perambulator with an elderly lady looking back from near the farmhouse the baby is Miss Rose Hartley, granddaughter to Inness, the elderly lady is Mrs. Hallock due to the slavery issue, many suffragettes put women's rights on hold and worked tirelessly to right the wrongs of slavery. Indeed several homes in Marlborough, by legend, were stations in the underground railroad. The Quakers especially were supportive of the equality of the races. Mary Hallock Foote (A Victorian Gentlewoman in the Far West, Henry E. Huntington Library and Art Gallery, 1972) remembers, "The women were for the most part silent, but not Aunt Sarah! She was Uncle Edward Hallock's second wife, a comparatively young woman when he died. She had no children and her stepsons were married men. With half her life's energies unspent she gave herself to books and gardening and friendship and reform. At intervals, between 1856 and the Civil War, we were visited by missionary lecturers sent forth by the New York Anti-slavery Society. Aunt Sarah, who belonged to the society, invited them,... and they were the guests of the Hallocks at large."

The New York Anti Slavery society was organized at a convention held in Utica in 1835, with Mary Hallock Foote's uncle, Townsend Hallock, as one of its vice-presidents. The object was the entire abolition of slavery in the United States. Townsend Hallock was brother-in-law to Sarah Hull Hallock.

Other guests of the Hallocks included Frederic Douglas and Harriet Beecher Stowe, author of "Uncle Tom's Cabin". In the description of the painting "On the Farm, Milton, NY" it is written, "Another of the rarely intimate pictures painted by the artist on the estate of Mrs. Asia Hallock at Milton, where writers, among them Harriet Beecher Stowe, and artists gathered during the summers of the eighties."(American Art Assoc., op. cit.) Harriet Beecher Stowe, daughter of a well known Congregational minister, was sister to Henry Ward Beecher, also a well known and influential minister of Plymouth Church in Brooklyn. Henry Ward Beecher was an admirer and proponent of George Inness. Perhaps this was the connection that first brought Inness to Milton.

A Legend Reborn

His had the wizened countenance of one who had spent many of his years in the out of doors, yet when we hit the woods he became a young jackrabbit scrambling over familiar rocks and hilly spots as if he had done so ever so many times before. He knew the face of that mountain as one would know the face of one's mother. As we walked he regaled us with stories of Bully's cave, Slaughterer's gulch and indeed the very spot where Bully is reputed to have been buried. Legend gained life.

We had moved to the top of the mountain several years before and now my cousins were negotiating with old Jack Ferguson to buy a piece of woodland that would become the "14 Acres". The Fergusons had been on top of the mountain since the early 1870s. Since the trip to town was long and arduous, they had to be fairly self supportive and there developed a small community of neighbors. Frank Nicklin (he'll be sadly missed) once told the story of one of the neighbors who, in the middle of the night snuck out to his neighbor's to steal some eggs only to return home and find several of his own chickens gone. There is a spot on top of Mt. Zion that, even though on top of the mountain is in a low spot and thus was called Scott's Hollow. There was a foundation there. As a kid I was quite surprised to find, still blooming in the spring, some daffodils and lilacs - planted lo those many years before at the threshold of someone's home.

I had thought we were at the "end of the world", the last house on top of Mt. Zion. Not so, in the woods were to be found several old foundations, or what was left of old foundations, testimony to the fact that others had lived and loved and died on top of that old mountain. Indeed, Mt. Zion is one of the oldest roads in Marlborough. It goes from Lattingtown Road to the top of the mountain with branches that once led all the way across the mountain to Lattingtown in one direction and in another, to Plattekill.

You can imagine how my interest was piqued when I got a call recently requesting information regarding a family that lived on top of Mt. Zion the second half of the 19th century. The caller was Al Rhodes, formerly from the

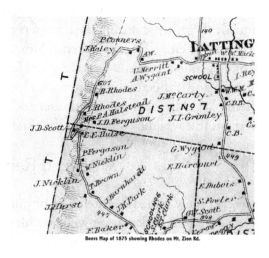

Beers Map of 1875 showing Rhodes on Mt. Zion Rd.

area - his mother lives in Bailey's Gap - but presently living in Florida. He said he was looking for the birthplace of his grandfather, Jonah Rhodes, who was born on "top of Mt. Zion" in the mid 1800s. Al was born in 1955 at Bailey's Gap, his father, Teddy, was born in 1906. His grandfather was Jonah born in 1872; his great grandfather Isaiah born in 1849 and his great, great grandfather was Daniel born in 1826. Al was coming into town and we agreed to meet.

I was able to find reference to Isaiah on an 1875 Beers Map and it clearly shows I. (Isaiah) Rhodes on top of Mt. Zion with a B. Rhodes just up the road. (see map)

Next, the censuses were checked.

1870 Census - Eliza J 67; Harriet (cousin) 64; Isaiah 29, Bloomer 24, Abbey J 20 - all Mt. Zion

1865 Census - Eliza 58 widow with 3 children; Isaiah 16; Jas. R. 20; Thomas (Bloomer) 18

1855 Census - Daniel 45 (42 yrs. in Marlborough) Eliza J 42; Isaiah 6; James 10; Thomas

1850 Census - Dan'l 40 laborer; Eliza J 36; James 5; Thomas B 3 and Isaiah 1

1840 Census - Daniel is also found with other members in his household, but, in the earlier censuses only the head of household and not other individuals in the family are named.

Then the land records were checked and I find the piece that Isaiah Rhodes sold in 1871 -"$50 - Commencing at a point in the highway a few rods south of the bridge over the outlet of Levi Crosby's swamp..." Levi Crosby, the blacksmith from Lattingtown, owned my brother's place (Bill Hennekens) beginning in 1830. I believe the land, part of Graham's Patent, was originally owned by a Rhodes. Isaiah bought the land back again and it went in and out of his family for a number of years. At one time later it also belonged to the Ferguson family.

Al Rhodes and his son, Alex, and I met and exchanged information. I found him to be very personable and we were both excited about the connections with Mt. Zion. We went first to an old foundation I had found in my earlier years that I believe to be a Rhodes foundation. It is in a briar filled woods just off the road. One would never expect to find a house there as the woods are grown all around.

Next we went just down the road to the piece of property that Isaiah sold in 1871. There is no old foundation on the property but we did explore "the outlet of Levi Crosby's swamp". The outlet, which flows under the road, is channeled under a crude stone bridge. One can only wonder at the age of the bridge as, to my knowledge, no work has been done on this small bridge in the remembered past. I do recall as a youngster traipsing through the woods and being enthralled by the "Silver leafs" we found growing next to the small brook. I don't know the name of the plant but I do know if you hold the leaf underwater with the bottom side up, it possesses a quicksilver look and quality - probably caused by air trapped under the leaf but who recognized that back then?

Al Rhodes at gravestone 2005

Our final stop was the alleged gravestone of Bully Rhodes - I think his real name was Billy and he held quite a reputation in that neighborhood. This is the gravestone that Jack Ferguson had pointed out as belonging to Bully almost 60 years ago. Is it Bully's final resting place? One can only wonder, but lacking substantial evidence to the contrary, this will always be, to the romantics amongst us, the final chapter in the legend of Bully Rhodes.

Father of Modernism

In 1877 the Caywoods bought a piece of property bordering on Buckley's Bridge. They later established "Shady Brook Farm", a boarding house. In the early 1920's one of the frequent guests was Alfred Maurer. Maurer, born in 1868, was the son of Louis, a highly successful graphic artist for Currier and Ives. He spent his early adult years in Paris studying art. He knew and was a guest at times of Gertrude Stein and her circle. He returned to the US just before the outbreak of WW1. Alfred Maurer was known as the "Father of Modernism" in American painting.

Maurer Self Portrait

It has been reported he was "artistically light years ahead" of his time. He has had a loyal following ever since. He painted a number of works while in Marlboro including one of Buckley's Bridge.

TITLE: Marlboro Landscape (Bridge)

ARTIST: Alfred Henry Maurer

WORK DATE: 1920

Buckley's Bridge

Of Families

The Measure of a Man

I never knew Stephen Case; neither did any of you. He died in Marlborough and left behind his last Will and Testament which was proved August 13, 1792. Interestingly, it was Shakespeare who said, "the good that men do is often interred with their bones." Somehow, through his gifts and his thoughtfulness, his words reach over the centuries and touch us even today, an indication that his good works live beyond his interment.

CASE, STEPHEN MARLBOROUGH Aug. 13, 1792 (abstracted)

(It is my desire) to be buried in decent Christian form...but not in an expensive way

If I die within 10 miles of New Marlborough church, it is my desire to be interred near my dear brother and two daughters "moulding in the dust there"

I leave my wearing apparel to my four sons - John, Weeler, Gabriel & Whitfield

My books and pamphlets equally divided among my three daughters - Esther Cropsey, Jane Franklin Case, and Charlotte Case - praying they may have the grace given them to read them carefully through

If there is any remaining estate after paying my just debts, it is to be divided equally between my loving wife, Glorianna Case and children - John, Wheeler, Gabriel, Whitfield, Ester Cropsey, Jane Franklin Case and Charlotte Case - £50 each

If after paying debts and the above bequests there is money still remaining, I bequeath £20 to New Marlborough Church

£10 for repairs to church and church yard

£10 to be given to a poor orphan or fatherless children whose fathers may have lost their lives in the service to their country in the late war with Great Britain.

John Wilkins, Esq. Attorney Goshen; Kindman (nb think he

means kin man - relative) Phenias Case, Goshen; and Major George D Wickham and Glorianna, my wife named Executors.

The greatest earthly benefactor that ever I had, exclusive of my parents, Wm. Wickham Esq., one of the judges of the Court of Common Pleas, Orange County - the overseer of my estate

Wit - Robert Blair, Dan'l Rudyard, Thurston Wood Aug. 13, 1792

Proved Sept. 21, 1797 - Gabriel Case appointed Administrator

The Will is a reminder that, even after the American Revolution, the legal currency of New York State was still the pound (£). Other reminders found in the Will include:

Transportation was not easy. Thus only if he died close enough to be transported with relative ease, did he state he wanted to be buried in the New Marlborough church cemetery (NB the Presbyterian cemetery on 9W).

He was FRUGAL! - "but not in an expensive way."

He wanted to be buried near his brother and two daughters who predeceased him - family plots have been in existence for many years

Clothing was a big issue then. It was very usual for people to will their clothing to next of kin - even the wealthiest did so.

Books and pamphlets were hard to come by, and quite expensive with the result that they became family treasures. Interestingly, he prays that his daughters "have the grace given them to read them carefully through."

As is still true today, there was a bequeath to the church. He displays his compassion by granting money to a poor orphan - reminding us that the Revolution, which had ended not many years before his death, took its toll on young fathers.

He displays great respect and affection for William Wickham who was a man of political power in the area during that period, at one time owning land in Marlborough.

No, I have never known Stephen Case, but in reading his Will, the essence of the man emerges. One can conjure up the man he was. I recognize his contribution to the character of our community, and, I do believe I would both like and respect the man were he alive today.

It's All Relative

I had gotten an e/mail a while ago from Richard and Sunny McMullen of Woodland Hills, CA. He was searching for the marriage certificate of his gggrandfather, Mathew McMillan of Scotland to Ann Hall of Ulster Co., NY in 1851. Finding records for this time frame is usually quite difficult.

Usually, the first place someone would look would be in the vital records maintained by the town clerk. Natalie Felicello has been most cooperative with such searches of the records, but she cannot provide what does not exist. New York State first required towns to keep records in 1847 - primarily for school purposes. There was a need to know of new students being born into the district. Only birth and death records were kept. Marlborough, but not all municipalities, kept faithful records (though not complete) for approximately three years. The State never collected the records and so municipalities stopped keeping them. The state did not thereafter require vital records be kept until the early 1870s and thus that is when, in most cases, vital records in New York state begin. Chances of finding a marriage record for the year 1851 were pretty meager.

The second place one usually would search for such a record would be in church registers. Alas, again Marlborough Church records are on the slim side. Many of our early church records either don't exist, or can't be found.

I turned to the census and indeed, did find several McMillens listed. In the 1855 NY census in family #169 was Ann McMillen age 21 born in Dutchess County with son Matthew McMillen 1 year - he was listed as a resident of Marlborough for 6 months. They are listed as living with Benson Hall 54, born in Dutchess, his wife, Eve, and daughter, Elizabeth, age 10. Benson is also found on the 1865 census at 65 years with wife, Eva, 64 years old, both born in Dutchess County, and Lizzie of 20 years born in Ulster County. For both censuses there were other Halls listed for Marlborough.

It was surprising to find on the 1855 NY Census a John Hall, 6 years of age, an orphan. The surprising part was he was living with Hilly and Eliza Fin, brother and sister, and Mary Griffen. In the household the only other persons were 12 orphans between the ages of 4 years and 10 years of age. Did Milton have a small orphanage in 1855?

Checking the web I found the family of John "Benson" Hall born 1800 in Clove (Dutchess County); his wife, Eva Dennis born 1802 in Dutchess County and children:

Egbert Benson Hall b 1819 Clove d 1888 Marlboro

Isaac Hall b 1821 Clove d 1890 m Sarah Gracy

Jane b 1823 married John H Baxter;

Ann b 1832 Clove d 1918 married Matthew McMullen b 1829 d 1890

and Sarah "Elizabeth" b 1844 Clove.

Then checking deeds I found:

in 1855 John H Baxter and Jane his wife sell 1A (House & lot) to Benson Hall

in 1861 Benson Hall & Eve, his wife sell 1/4A to Sarah Hall, wife of Isaac

in 1864 Elizabeth Staples, wife of Samuel sells to Sarah Hall, wife of Isaac 3.43A

in 1869 Sarah Hall, wife of Isaac (Fishkill) sells to Benson Hall the above 3.43A

in 1877 Benson Hall & wife Eve sell to Caroline Hall, wife of Harrison 1/4A

in 1877 Benson Hall & wife, Eve sell to Caroline Hall, wife of Harrison 3.43A

in 1883 Caroline Hall of Bloomfield, NJ sells to Eugene Covert 3.5A

in 1886 Covert sells the same land back to Caroline Hall of Bloomfield, NJ

(interestingly on this deed for Caroline it mentions - "By occupation - a lady)

in 1891 Caroline Hall of Glen Ridge, NJ sells the 3.5A to Patrick Manion

Eugene Covert was the husband of Rhoda Ann Hall, sister to Benson Hall.

I sent this material to Richard and was pleased to find out he was planning a venture to our area in order to "search out his roots." We met for lunch at the Raccoon Saloon, which at one time was owned and operated as the Farmers' Hotel by Moses McMullen. We don't know if there was any connection with Richard's McMullen line, but they were pleased with the possibility, and the lunch, as usual, was excellent. They enjoyed the view of the Hudson River and the falls and "Sucker" hole. We shared the information we both had gathered.

Our first stop was to the town hall to check records (after 1870)

for some Halls that Richard believed had died in Marlborough. Again, Natalie was most cooperative. We did find several records of interest for example, Egbert Hall's death certificate Dec. 2, 1888 - Egbert was brother to Jane Hall McMullen. Interestingly, we could find no records of burials in the Marlborough area.

Next stop was out towards West Marlborough near the Greiner farm to the spot where Benson Hall had once lived with his family. I had spoken with George Greiner and he indicated there had been a house at that spot until a relatively short number of years ago.

An interesting aside - the deed of April 1, 1864 from Elizabeth Staples to Sarah Hall, wife of Isaac (3.43 acres) there is mention "east 5 chains 67 links to the center of a certain new road that was laid through said lands in 1861" - "Reserving the privilege for the public of opening said new road and occupying a strip of 1.5 rods wide off the east side of the above premises for the purpose of a public highway." In 1869 Sarah sells the same piece to Benson Hall and mentioned is, "Bounded on the north by the 'Ola' road." Thus we also get a view into the changes made in Plattekill Road in 1861 as well as one of the old road names.

We then did a quick tour of the town as they were very interested in seeing where their forebears had once lived. They continued to do research in the area, specifically in Clove in Dutchess County.

Richard & Sunny McMullen in front of Raccoon Saloon - one time owned and operated by Moses McMullen

53

When they got back to California, they spent quite a bit of time pulling together the information they had gained on their trip. They were kind enough to share their information with me. It seems the grand-father of our Benson Hall, was Benjamin Hall born 1740 in Rhode Island who came to Dutchess County in 1750. He signed the Articles of Association in Beekman and from 1776 to 1783 served in the American Revolution. The McMullens are currently applying for membership in the DAR. Richard says the Halls were a famous Beekman Patent land grant family of Dutchess County. While the Halls lived in Marlborough for a period of time, they tended to go back to Dutchess County for their burials, thus we were not able to find any in the Marlborough area.

Now, at this point you're probably thinking, "O.K., interesting, but the Halls were in Marlborough for such a relatively short period of time". The Halls married into the Covert family, the Baxter family, and the McMullen family (though this tie to our McMullens is tenuous). These families have branches that reach into the Fowlers, the Hallocks, the Mackeys, the McElraths, the Stewarts, the Atkins, the Clarks, the Nicklins, the Palmateers and the Partingtons - and, I probably have missed a few! If the truth were to be known, they're probably related to half the town.

Faith of our Fathers

It's always been one of my favorite hymns, especially when sung with gusto. It seems to capture the feeling of a book recently written by Carol Felter entitled "Wygant Grandfathers". The book is a chronicle of nine generations of Wygants who have enriched the Marlborough story.

Carol was not content just going back to the early 1700's, she starts her story about the time of the Reformation with a possible tie-in to Bishop John Wigand born in Mansfeld, Saxony in the year 1523. She has done a lot of research and presents much interesting historical background of the Reformation, the "Black Death of 1666", the 30 Year War, and the following generations of Wygants in Germany.

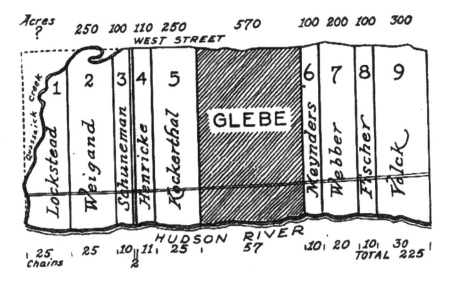

Final Allotment of Land in the German Patent of 1719.
(Western Line Now Conforms to Line of River.)

The first Wygant to step foot on American soil was Michael who, with his family, was part of the Palatines who sailed with their pastor, the Reverend Joshua Kockerthal in 1709 to Newburgh, NY there to set up a new home and a new life in the new world. Carol gives a good account of this early Palatine settlement that would become the Newburgh we know today. Michael Wynant is on the 1718-19 Tax list for the High Lands (which included Newburgh, Marlborough and other areas) as paying 15£. His land was later developed and part of it became Washington's Headquarters on Liberty Street. One son of Michael Wygant was Tobias whose son Martin was the proprietor of Weigand Tavern, a rallying place for patriots during the Revolutionary War. A second Weigand's Tavern, built by Martin, still exists on Liberty Street in Newburgh.

Wygant's Tavern Newburgh, NY
(still standing)

A second son of Michael Weigant was George (Uri) who in 1723 married Jane Bond.

Jane Bond was one of three daughters of Captain William Bond. William Bond was quite an influential man who was able to acquire a good bit of land in the Marlborough area. In 1710 Bond was granted "The Bond Patent" of 600 acres which is the southern part of Milton. He also got a grant for 500 acres in Plattekill (which was then part of Marlborough), just over the present boundary between Marlborough and Plattekill on Milton Turnpike referred to as "Ten Stones Meadow". In 1714 Bond was one of the recipients of a tract of land known as the Morris Patent which is the center of Marlborough from above Lattingtown to the Orange County line. Since the Patent was granted to seven men it has been referred to as the "Seven Patentees". William Bond died in 1740. The Bond portion of the Seven Patentee's Patent was willed to Bond's three daughters and eventually became the property of the Wygant. Uri and Jane settled in Marlboro in 1744 and started the Wygant farming tradition in Marlborough. Thus the first generation of Marlborough farming Wygants was George Wygant (Uri).

Mikel was the son of Uri who inherited most of Uri's land, his brother, William, having received a grant of 100 acres in the Bond Patent (in Milton) from his aunt, Sukie (Susannah Bond). Mikel was 18 when his family moved from Newburgh to Marlborough. He was a sheep rancher and Carol does a good job explaining the importance of sheep to the early settlers - most, if not all of their clothing was homespun. Mikel gave money to support the first subscription to the Presbyterian Church in Marlboro and in 1764 the first Presbyterian Church in Ulster County was built just south of DiDonato's Funeral Home. There is a historic marker on 9W denoting the church's location. Carol has quite a bit on the early church history as well.

Mikel married Rebecca Presler. Mikel is believed to have been the builder of the Baxter House on the corner of Plattekill Road and South Street. In 1775, Mikel at 49 years of age, with 223 others in Marlborough, signed the Articles of Association - by which he pledged:

"We ...shocked by the bloody scene now acting in Massachusetts Bay (The Battle of Concord and Lexington), do in the most solemn manner resolve never to become slaves, and do associate under all the ties of religion, honor and love of our country to adopt and endeavor to carry into execution whatever measures may be recommended by the Continental Congress... "

How stirring still are those words that have reverberated for over 200 years of American history. Mikel and two of his sons enlisted in the service leaving the oldest son, John, to run the farm.

In her book Carol quotes from an article by Ann Landers a number of years ago when Landers explained the consequences possible for those who had signed the Declaration of Independence. Landers wrote of several including Thomas Nelson Jr.:

At the Battle of Yorktown, Thomas Nelson Jr. noted that the British Gen. Cornwallis had taken over the Nelson home for his headquarters. He quietly urged Gen. Washington to open fire. The home was destroyed, and Nelson died bankrupt.

A similar fate was recognized as possible for any of those called "Patriots" in America and "Rebels" in England.

In 1784 Mikel was one of the nine trustees chosen by the Presbyterian Church. Mikel died in 1807 leaving his land to his sons. Thus Mikel was the second generation Marlborough farmer.

Mikel left part of his land to his son, Matthew (who Carol calls "Teefus"). Matthew, also was a sheep rancher and an officer in the Presbyterian Church. He was 18 when, with his father and brothers, signed the Articles of Association. Shortly thereafter he enlisted in Lewis DuBois's Regiment of the militia. He married Sarah Waring and settled on land his father had given him on Lattingtown Road (later to become the Rapisardi property). Matthew was the third generation Marlborough farmer.

Matthew's son, James, was born in 1787 and fought in the War of 1812. In 1816 he married Philena Waring. James bought 100 acres from Nathaniel Belly and James and Philena set up household in what is presumed to be the old Belly house. This was to become for the next several generations "The Wygant Farm". James pioneered the raising of grapes in the 1850s. He, like his forebears was a trustee in the Presbyterian Church. James was the forth generation Marlborough farmer.

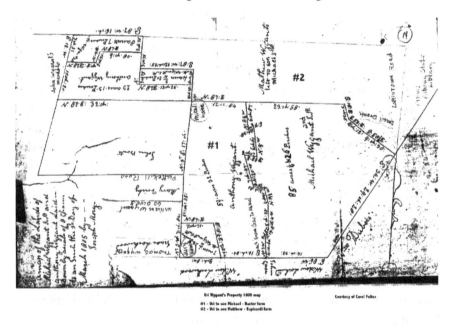

Uri Wygant's Property 1805 map
#1 - Uri to son Michael - Baxter farm
#2 - Uri to son Matthew - Rapisardi farm

Courtesy of Carol Felter

Faith of our Fathers (Part II)

In the last story we covered the first four generation of Wygant farmers in Marlborough. Uri married to Jane Bond who was the first and settled near the Baxter farm. Mikel, who inherited most of Uri's land, married Rebecca Presler and it is believed built the Baxter House.

He, like his father was a sheep farmer. Matthew (Teefus) was the third Wygant farmer in Marlborough and also a sheep farmer. He married Sarah Waring. The fourth was James Wygant, who married Philena Waring, and pioneered the raising of grapes in the 1850s.

Clemence Wygant was born in 1820. Clemence attended school at the old one-room school house near Schwartz's bridge. The school is no longer there, but was just west of the bridge over Old Man's Creek - the intersection of Western Avenue and Lattingtown Road. The school, as described in Carol Felter's book was originally a log cabin with a wood burning stove for heat and the, at that time, standard bucket of water and dipper. The desk was a long board with wooden seats. Carol relates, "They sometimes played 'squeeze' by pushing and pushing until the end pupil fell off in the midst of his reciting". Ethan Parrot is named as one of the teachers in this old school.

Clemence saw the transition from sheep farming to fruit farming, though part of the Wygant farm is still referred to as the "sheep pen". Family stories tell of using sheep to run the treadmill used to grind corn. Grapes, introduced by James, were quite profitable. Clemence introduced other fruits also. It was the time when Marlborough became famous due to the Antwerp Raspberry.

In 1854 Clemence married Sarah Young, a Quaker from a New York City family. Shortly thereafter the Civil War erupted. In 1864 Clemence and Sarah named one of their sons Elmer Ellsworth Wygant after the first northerner to die in the Civil War. Carol reports that Clemence did not go to war, "because he had lost his front teeth and couldn't bite the cap off the bullet". That was also the year Clemence's father James died.

Clemence enlarged the original house on the property and moved his young family into it. In 1865 Calvin became the first child to be born in the newly expanded house. It was also the end of the Civil War and the time of the assassination of Abraham Lincoln. This family of Wygants, like their predecessors, attended the Presbyterian Church which at this time was on Main Street (presently 9W). In 1869 the church burned down with only a Bible and a marble topped table salvaged. There followed a time of fund raising in order to build a new church. Clemence was a generous subscriber. Carol reports on the picnic that was held at Clark's Basket Factory grounds where the last of the $33,000 needed for the new church was raised. The new church was built again on DuBois lands but now a block from the highway.

Clemence was quite a real estate venturer and, at the time of his death in 1902, owned at least fourteen houses and several small farms in Marlborough.

(John) Calvin, son of Clemence, was born in 1863. In 1890 he married Charlotte Barnes and was given, by his father Clemence, land that he developed between Western Avenue and Church Street in Marlborough. He built his house (presently Esposito's home) and a barn and an icehouse. There was also a tennis court. He ran a small farm there.

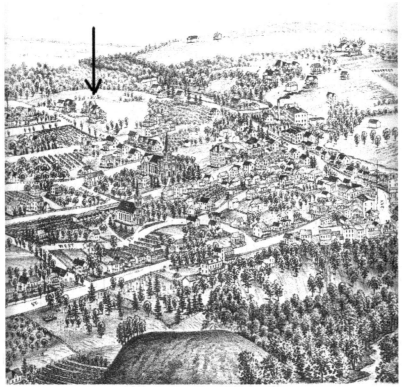

J. C. Wygant new house & farm - 1891 Marlborough Map

Upon the death of Clemence, he bought his brothers' shares and became owner of the family farm. He continued to live in the village, daily driving his horse and wagon to the farm. In 1905 a fire destroyed the barn and cold storage at his village farm.

Wygant Family Farm - Lattingtown Road

In 1906 he was elected president of the village and served for two terms. Yes, at one time there was an entity known as Marlboro Village with a board and officers separate from the town. During his term the village saw the first municipal electric lights, municipal water and sidewalks. The Marlborough Water Works Company had been formed in 1893 to supply water to the town and to the railroad from the reservoir to the west. The water flowed by gravity from the reservoir to the town. Phillip T. Schantz was president of the Water Works Company and in 1912 the company sold out to the village of Marlborough for $30,000. This was the primary source of water for the town for many years until the hookup with the New York City water supply. At the "old" railroad station there was a water tower that serviced the steam engines.

J. Calvin died in 1948. His obituary reads, in part,:

Mr. Wygant was a pioneer in fruit raising and introduced many new varieties of fruit in this section including the McIntosh apple. A progressive, scientific farmer, Mr. Wygant's farm was often the site for new, experimental methods of fruit raising directed by the Farm Bureau. He also built the first cold storage plant in Marlborough.

J Calvin was the sixth generation of Wygant farmers in Marlborough.

Faith of our Fathers (3)

James Calvin was born in 1895. He was one of three, and the president, of the first graduating class of Marlboro High School in 1914. His daughter, Carol was finishing 6th grade when the school was closed.

His sister, Marion was a few years older and so had to go to Newburgh to high school. Each morning she walked from her home on Church Street to the Marlborough train station, took the train to Newburgh and walked up the hill in Newburgh to the school. The trip was the opposite in the late afternoon for her return.

Carol reports that when James Calvin was a youngster, he walked every day, before school, to the family farm (on Lattingtown Road) to check on traps he had set for fur bearing animals.

In 1918 James Calvin discovered his family had had him deferred from the war (WWI) because of working the family farm. He went to New Paltz and registered. He served in France but the war ended before he was sent to the front line. He later became a charter member of the Viebey Sutton Post of the American Legion.

In 1920 and 1921 Cal spent the winter with Ted Baker in Florida near the Sutcliffs. The Sutcliffs ran the shoddy mill at Prospect and White Streets. The shoddy mill burned down.

James Calvin was married in 1923 to Ernestine Cole, a young Marlboro High School teacher. Ernestine had come to Marlboro a short time before to begin her teaching duties and was living with Dr. and Mrs. Taylor across the street from the Wygants (in the Plank house). Dr. Taylor was the high school principal at the time. James Calvin built the present Wygant home on Hudson Terrace just west across the street from his father's home.

In that same year, his father, John Calvin, turned over the primary responsibility of the family farm and began spending his winters in Florida.

In 1935 the barn on the family farm was struck by lightening. It was replaced with a cooler and packing house that was enlarged again in the 1960s.

James Calvin and Ernestine did extensive traveling in Europe, Africa, Ireland, South America and Australia. James Calvin died in 1970. He was the seventh generation of Wygant farmers in Marlborough.

James Calvin, Jr. (Cal) was born in 1932. He had perfect attendance in elementary junior and senior high school. (Though with his humor, Cal said he wouldn't do that again!). He achieved the Eagle rank in the Boy Scouts. He graduated from Dartmouth College and began his career as farmer on the Wygant family farm. He was secretary of the Milton Marlboro Medical Building Association. The association was established to attract a doctor into the town as, at the time, there was none. The association was responsible for building the medical building on 9W.

In 1955 Cal married Jane Rusk. The couple had children Amy, George and Polly.

Like his father and his grandfather, Cal traveled daily from the village to the farm. Cal enlarged the cold storage plant on the farm as well as increased the acreage under cultivation. In October of 1989 Cal received a Certificate of Recognition from the Assistant Secretary of Agriculture that read:

> In this the 200th anniversary year of the U.S. Constitution, the U.S. Department of Agriculture is pleased to acknowledge the vital contribution of farm families to the growth and strength of this great Nation. Your farm has been recognized as having been in the same family since the birth of the U.S. Constitution.

Befittingly, Cal also served as President of the Marlborough Historical Society.

Cal, the eighth generation of Wygant farmers in Marlborough died in 2001. The farm has now passed into the hands of his children.

The author, Carol Felter, at her favorite pastime, feeding the ducks and fish at Mariner's Harbor

This writer has barely touched the high points in the Wygant story. Carol Felter's book, "Wygant Grandfathers", goes into much detail, not only of the Wygant family, but of the ambiance of the times in which they lived. There is much Marlborough history there. Readers are encouraged to discover for themselves by reading the book.

Uri Wygant first settled in Marlborough with his wife and ten children - they all being the first Wygants to dwell in Marlborough. On the 1790 census there were 49 Wygants listed and on the 1865 there were 65 Wygants. Today there is but one Wygant family listed in the Marlborough phone book, BUT...since many of the Wygant females married into other families, Wygant blood still flows through many a vein in Marlborough.

Since Mikel first made his subscription to the Presbyterian Church in Marlborough, Wygants have been leaders and strong supporters of the church. Today Wygant descendants play a major role in the church. "Faith of our Fathers living still......."

Young at Heart 1

What does it mean to be "Young at Heart"? For members of a Marlborough family that phrase has special meaning.

This story starts about 1755 or 1756 when John Young arrived on the American shores from England. He settled on Long Island and shortly thereafter married Dorcus Hallock, daughter of Edward. Edward was desirous of settling in Marlborough on land he had recently purchased and so sent his son-in-law, John Young, and his daughter to pave the way. In the middle of the winter of 1760 Edward and his wife and ten children were greeted by John and Dorcus Young when they first stepped off Hallock's open sailing vessel onto "Forefather's Rock" in Milton near the foot of Old Indian Road. Local legend is that first winter all fourteen of them lived in a modest 14' x 20' building with an upper alcove for sleeping near the Lewis House on South Road in Milton. What discomforts they suffered that first winter can only be imagined, but the families stayed and thrived.

They were of the Quaker religion and soon a modest Quaker enclave was evidenced in Marlborough with the center being the Milton area.

Edward Hallock, father-in-law to John Young, bought 155 acres from Richard Woolsey in the Kennedy Patent of 800A. This is land near Lyons Lane - on both sides of the highway. In 1766 Edward Hallock sold this land to John Young.

Edward Young, son of John and Dorcus was born Jul 23, 1775 in Marlborough during the Revolutionary period. As a Quaker he was very antislavery and adhered to the Temperance movement. It is believed the Youngs were part of the Underground Railroad that was evidenced in Milton. Edward was responsible for the liberation of two slaves who had been sold into bondage from New York State.

Edward married Hannah Halstead of Dutchess County. According to Beers (Commemorative Biographical Record of Ulster County 1896) her mother was a Cromwell, reputedly a descendant of Oliver Cromwell, "The Protector." In 1810 Edward started a private boarding school in Milton

When John Young died c1808, he willed much of the land from the Kennedy Patent to his son, Edward.

According to Beers, Edward was the first man in the township to engage in fruit raising and the first to sell apple trees in Marlborough. He also came into possession of some very special raspberry plants and introduced the Antwerp Raspberry to the area. He is credited with creating a market for the raspberry in New York City. Some have claimed that it was the Antwerp Raspberry that put Marlborough on the map.

Edward kept adding land to his original farm until at one point he owned over 300 acres and was improved to the extent that it became one of the finest in the county. The improvements according to Beers were:

The rocks were taken out and made into stone fences that stand straight to this day, monuments to his enterprise; ditches were dug and filled and uneven places smoothed over, he sometimes keeping as many as 40 men in his employ. The houses and barns were built as they now (1896) are today with the exception of one that was burned.

Beers goes on to indicate the mansion, occupied by Fred W Vail (a grandson of Edward's) was planned and built under Edward's supervision, as was also the barn on Smith Young's (another grandson of Edward's) farm and many others.

Edward and Hannah Young had five sons: John born 1803 (more of him later); David born 1808; Alexander born 1810; Edward born 1814 and William C. born 1815.

Edward purchased a large tract of land in Hampton (just South of the Marlborough border) and had a large farm there. When Edward died in 1855, the main portion of this farm fell into the hands of two of his sons, Alexander and William C.

Alexander and William C. married two sisters, Deborah Ann and Althea Harcourt daughters of Benjamin Harcourt who also owned much land in Marlborough. Benjamin died circa 1866 and left most of his land to his sons. He did, however, leave both of his daughters Deborah and Althea $2,000 - which in 1866 must have been a goodly sum. For about fifteen years Alexander and William C., and their wives, lived on the Hampton farm - apparently in the same household.

In 1856 William C. bought a large portion of the formerly Lewis DuBois property in Marlborough. A year or so later he built a dock there, known as the "Upper Dock" and engaged in selling coal, feed and other products. The steamer, "Queen of Wappingers Falls" was the first boat to land at his dock. He was also an agent for the Romer & Tremper & Cornell Steamboat Co. until 1891. It was during this time that the dock area was so busy with farmers shipping their produce to New York City by boat.

According to Cochrane the sand bank to the north of the dock used to come all the way almost to the river. To William C. Young "belongs the credit of digging away a large part of it." It is believed that William C had a "shoot" near the old West Shore Railroad depot and ran cord wood to the river.

In 1884 William C took his son, Charles (born in 1848 in Cedar Cliff) into partnership, under the name of WC Young & Son. According to Cochrane (1887) the cut off road to the dock was built through the efforts of William C as the only road of record from the village to the docks. The lower end was the property of the West Shore RR Co.

At an earlier time there was a steam ferry operating from Young's Dock to Hampton and New Hamburg on the other side of the river.

Speaking of a later time, in an interview with Tom Pollizzi a few years ago Tom spoke of helping to load the boats. He was a young lad and youngsters were paid a penny a basket for loading the fruit. Tom also spoke of the long lines of cars and trucks lined up all along Dock Road waiting to be

Charles Young.

unloaded. Vehicles often had to back up Dock Road as it was so steep, the motors would conk out if not driven backwards.

Charles Young, son of William C. married Marion Pect in 1882. These Youngs had three children: Ralph P, William C. and Adelaide T.

The Marlborough hose company was incorporated in 1897. One of the early members was Ralph Young. In the 1920's Ralph Young was one of those largely responsible for the building of the Marlborough Library (on the corner of King and Main Street). The library replaced the old "flatiron" building which Plank (1959) called "the ancient wooden monstrosity".

Adelaide (Young) Traphagen sold the land of the Marlborough Yacht Club. Plank says, land "which has seen the days of sail, the earliest days of steam and the later building of the railroad". He goes on to say "where now are only rotted timbers the Young dock reached out over the river until recent years and until the twenties was a busy place when the steamers came in."

The Youngs also owned the land upon which the Railroad station was built and land upon which the present Marlboro Middle and Marlboro Elementary schools sit.

Young at Heart II

What does it mean to be Young at heart? Last article explored that question with information about the earliest Youngs in the town of Marlborough - the first being John Young (1). Information was provided about Edward Young, son of John (1) and Edward's sons Alexander and William C. Another son of Edward was John (2) born in 1803 and married to Martha Sands, Phebe Hallock and Rispah R Whitney. Of John Young (2) it was said, he "was known as the workingman's friend and to have risen from bed at night to take a basket of food to those whom he thought might be in want." (Beers, Commemorative Biographical Record of Ulster County, 1896).

His marriage to Phebe S Hallock produced a son, Smith Young born in 1833. There must at one time have been an early school on or near Sherman Drive in Milton as Beers reports that Smith Young first attended this school. Later Smith Young went to "read law" (clerk) under a Judge Fullerton in Newburgh. It was said he gave up law, "because he was too honest". Apparently he also attended debating school which Beers writes was more prevalent in his earlier days. The Youngs, before turning to fruit, had raised cattle and of Smith Young Beers writes, "A nice field of grain to him is a thing of beauty."

Smith Young married Jeannie S Wygant, daughter of James Wygant of Marlboro. Apparently Jeannie was well educated for those days as she completed a four year course at the Northrup boarding school in Marlboro. To this couple, in 1862, was born Edward Young. Edward attended the Turnpike school in Milton and then attended a private school kept by a Miss Johnson in the old Friends Church in Milton.

Milton Turnpike School Milton, NY Circa 1913

Top Row - L to R - Ellen Gersch, Al Tabr, Whalen McManus, Joe Matthews, Ed Young, Angelina Dirago, Rose Salzano, Theresa Garvey, Johanna McManus, Miss Smith (Teacher)

Middle Row - Jerry Casaburo, Rose Dirago, Jim Dirago, Eber Atkins, Wilbur Atkins, Bill Shay, Rocky Grundio, Oscar George Wendover, Joe Dirago, Ambrose McManus, Miss Perrine, Helen Connors, Mary Casaburo, Mary McManus, Ballet

Bottom row - Anna Fox, Sophie Gersch, Helen Taber, Jean Dirago, John Donovan, Millie Dirago, Mary D'Agostino, Catherine Casaburo, Antonette Dirago, Elizabeth Salzano, Loretta Donovan, Mike Grundio, Josephine Perrine

Edward was an advanced Mason. Edward, as was his forebears, was very active in the Friends Society and helped found the Christian Endeavor movement in the area. It was through this association with the Christian Endeavor movement that Edward met Eliza Keates, daughter of the Reverend Harry R Keates, a Friends minister. Eliza was born in England but moved with her family, first to Clintondale, and then to Milton where her youngest sibling was born. The Reverend Keates serving as Friends minister in both those communities.

Edward was very involved with his community serving as town supervisor for twenty years. According to family legend as passed down to Bob Young, grandson of Edward, Edward often would cross the

Hudson with horse and sleigh. One time he had just made it back to discover that someone from Highland had not been so lucky - they had gone through the ice. Though the man was saved, the horse was drowned. Perhaps this sparked his interest in having a bridge built between Highland and Poughkeepsie. He became an early advocate for the bridge and instrumental in having it built.

Eliza became very involved in the Women's Christian Temperance Union and in the Farm Bureau. She did extensive traveling with the Farm Bureau which included trips to Europe. According to Bob Young, there is a plaque at the State Fair grounds in Syracuse dedicated to Eliza Young and the services to farming that she contributed.

Edward and Eliza Young became friends with, the then NY State Governor, Franklin D Roosevelt and his wife, Eleanor. Eliza had had training to become a teacher under the London School Board. She had shown her organizational skills through her work for the Farm Bureau. Perhaps, in part, due to these factors, Eliza was appointed to the Committee of Twenty-one. It's my understanding that the Committee of Twenty-one was an ad-hoc committee appointed by FDR to study the need to improve education within the state by combining some of the smaller, less well-funded school districts into centralized districts. Marlborough is reputed to be one of the early centralized districts within the state. Befittingly, Eliza gave an address at the Dedication ceremonies of the new Milton Elementary School.

It is believed that Edward and Eliza accepted the invitation to attend the inauguration of Franklin D. Roosevelt as President. It is known that Eleanor Roosevelt did visit Eliza on several occasions. Bob Young remembers meeting Eleanor at his grandmother's home. She made him drink his milk.

Eleanor, for a number of years had been writing a newspaper column entitled, "My Day". On April 26, 1945, just two weeks after the death of FDR Eleanor wrote;

One of my friends whom I have not seen for some time — Mrs. Eliza Keates Young, who lives in the small rural community of Milton, just across the river from us — sent me a verse which may be a comfort to a great many whose dear ones are meeting death in the war. It reads:

"They are not dead who live in lives they leave behind: In those whom they have blessed they live a life again."

Apparently Eliza had had some prose and poetry published when she lived in England.

When the Milton Engine Company was organized in 1904, Edward Young was one of the trustees. When the incorporated village of Marlboro was dissolved in 1922, Edward Young was town supervisor. He appointed EC Quimby, Howard Kniff and Frank Snyder to act as trustees of the water system until a water district could be formed.

Beers (1896) reports that Edward and Eliza Keates Young had two children; Elizabeth born Dec 13, 1893 and Keates born May 11, 1895. Beers predates Edward Young who was born in 1897.

Young at Heart III

We've been exploring the question, "What does it mean to be Young at heart?" In the last few articles we've brought you up to Edward Young, son of Smith Young. and his family.

John Young, son of Edward, is remembered in the memoirs of Vin Russo. Apparently John was quite a fisherman. Vin writes, "We never had any store bought fishing equipment. We would make a pole out of a sapling and the line from grape twine. The hooks we got from some of the older guys that fished a lot. I got mine from John Young. John was Ed Young's brother. He was a great guy and was well liked by all the kids; he was good to us." Vin continues by saying he has gotten a lot of pleasure from fishing and now has wonderful memories - all thanks to John who was his mentor.

Bob Young indicated that Eleanor (Smith) Rosekranse & Elizabeth Smith, her sister, were both named after two of his aunts - daughters of Edward Young.

Keates Young, another son of Edward is given the credit for starting the Young's Fireworks that entertained so many on July 4th for a number of years. It was Keates and his mother, Eliza Keates Young, who first paid for the fireworks held in a large field near their home. Bob Young remembers having to clear the hay from the field prior to the big event each year. After the first year Anthony Russo and John Matthews (Jr.), neighbors, contributed money towards the fireworks and they became even bigger. Then Tony Andola and Frank Salzano added funds along with other in the community until the fireworks began to attract thousands of spectators. Bob Young thought the fireworks started in the early 1950s and ran until the late 60s or early 70s. The crowds eventually became so large that the fireworks were moved to Cluett Schantz Park.

Turnpike School c 1910
Ed Young holding flag

Edward Young, son of Edward, was born circa 1904. He is listed on the 1905 census as being 1 year old. He attended the Milton Turnpike school on the corner of Milton Turnpike and Clark's Lane. There are pictures of Edward and his class outside the building. The teacher was a Miss Smith. Interestingly, the names of the students have been preserved - except..... Note there is one black youngster in the picture. The only information about him is his nickname, "Bullet". Anyone with more information about him, please let me know. There is also another picture of Edward holding the flag as his classmates saluted during the morning orientation activities. These pictures are circa 1910 - 1913.

Bob Young ventured that his family had given the land for the

Turnpike School. In checking it out at the County Clerk's Office in Kingston I find: Sept. 21, 1852 (L84/P354) John Young, & Phebe S, his wife to James Sherman and Oscar Clark Trustees of School District #12 - $23.50 - to their successors in office as such trustees

On a part of which the school house of said District now stands

Beginning at Morgan S Dayton's corner of the highway leading S from the Turnpike and running thence W along said turnpike 100' near to a ledge of rocks; thence S parallel with the base of said ledge of rocks as a stone wall now stands made since the sale of said lot 150'; then E 100'; then N 140' to the place of beginning

This grant is upon the following conditions:

Parties of the second part and their successors as aforesaid are to fence the said lot on all sides and to keep said fence in sufficient repair as long as they possess the same

The parties of the first part, their heirs and assigns are to have the privilege of planting and cultivating in said lot ornamental or other trees as they see fit which trees shall not be cut down or injured by parties of the second part or their successors or by said District and whenever the said lot shall cease to be used for the purposes of a district school all the land with the trees upon it shall revert to the parties of the first part, their heirs or assigns free and discharged from this grant, but parties of the second part or their successors as aforesaid may remove from the premises any buildings which shall be put on or which are now on belonging to the District

Bob Young mentioned that family legend was that the land was to revert to the family and, indeed, such seems to be the case. Since the school is no longer on the lot (it closed at least by 1937 when the district was centralized) it can be argued that the School District is not using the property for school purposes. How about giving it back?

Besides attending the Turnpike School, Ed Young, as so many of the Youngs did, attended Oakwood Friends School. The school was founded in 1796 at Millbrook, NY by the Society of Friends, the first coeducational Friends boarding school in the country. The school moved to Poughkeepsie in 1920. Bob Young also attended Oakwood.

Young Edward early in his life worked on the family farm. Shortly thereafter, according to Bob, he and Claude Hepworth worked as bell hops, then as chauffeurs after which Ed started to work for Carl

Rhodes in Milton at the corner garage across from the post office. This, apparently, is where he picked up his mechanical abilities and honed his love for things automotive.

Young at Heart IV

It was in 1928 that Ed Young started his garage for repairing and servicing cars and trucks and, since he was then on the relatively new highway, for selling gasoline.

Vin Russo reports on the good work that Ed Young performed. Vin reports that one night someone stole "our old rust bucket truck". It was found the next day, but had been partially wrecked.

"Ed Young went down to pick it up with his wrecker. He repaired it rather quickly and it was back to work in no time". Young's had his own body man back then. In those days you didn't replace parts, they beat them back into shape. Well let me tell you when they got done with that fender it looked like new. It was the only body part that was not rotten or dented or rusted or scratched.

Today, if we didn't junk the whole truck, we would at least have to buy a new fender.

According to Bob Young, Ed Young also had the contract for sanding 9W from the county line to Esopus. He sanded with his dump truck and always made sure the kids could get home from school. Glen Clark, Sr., Jason Martin, Edgar Rhodes, Joey Dirago and (he thinks) Len Schreiber helped at various times. They used only the one truck and dumped the sand by shovel - it had to be a backbreaking job.

Young's Garage was also the terminal for Greyhound and Mt. View buses. The buses stopped right in front of the garage.

Edward Young was also very active in the local Lions Club. He was the chairman of the New York State Lions in 1952. He attended an international meeting of the Lions club held in Mexico City as New York State Representative. According to Bob, he drove all the way down and back.

In the 1960s Ed Young was a member of the Marlborough Central School Board. It was during his term that the new Marlboro Elementary School was built and dedicated.

Ed Young was also involved in minstrels held in town at St. James'

Hall. He and Pat Mataraza, Joe Pessavento and Joe Rossano, among others, were instrumental in having turkey dinners served to all the less fortunate kids in town.

Ed also was very active in the Fire Company in Milton. According to Bob, when the Fire Company couldn't afford the doors to the new fire house, Ed Young paid for the extra wide doors needed to accommodate the fire trucks. After the tragic accident in which the new fire truck was wrecked according to Vinnie Russo:

"The beautiful fire truck that everyone was so proud of was a complete and total wreck. Buying a new fire truck was out of the question. Besides the money, it would take months and months to get one. The nation was beginning to gear up for war.

So, Ed Young came to the rescue. He brought the truck to his garage and it became a high priority. His body man would work on it during the regular work day and Ed would work on it at night. He worked on that truck every night sometime until one or two in the morning, amazing. Finally, after several months, the truck was finished. It looked as good as it did before the wreck."

Vin Russo tells an amusing tale about his own father. Vin said his father was not mechanically inclined. When the elder Russo needed to repair something he would measure it between his fingers and then cross Milton Turnpike holding his fingers as steady as he could in order to ask for a wrench about the size he needed. Ed Young would get a big kick out of this and in order to accommodate this unique means of measuring wrenches, often lent Russo several wrenches until, finally, he decided to lend him an adjustable wrench.

Young's Garage had a tragic fire in 1938. According to Vin Russo, "I do remember it was winter time, because there was snow on the ground. That fire is burned into my memory." Vin lived just across the street from Young's Garage. Vin goes on to say, "A lesser man would have probably given up. It was the height of the depression, with no garage, no income and no money, Ed Young built a bigger and better garage and became a well respected Chrysler/Plymouth dealer."

Bob Young said the garage was burned to the ground and there was no insurance money. Some of their good neighbors including Carmine and Willie Palladino helped to rebuild the garage. However, when 9W was again widened, it was virtually impossible to pump gas from the gas pumps in front of the garage and Young's terminated the selling of gas.

Youngs have also played a significant part in the success of Little League in the area. Early on the likes of Joe Conroy would play ball on Young property. Indeed, with tongue in cheek, Vinnie Russo said, "The only flat spot in-Milton was Young's field where the men played baseball." Bob Young said it was many of the same men who helped to organize the fire works who later helped to organize and set up the Little League field. Youngs lease the present "Young's Field" to the town of Marlborough in order for the Little League to have fields on which to play. Every year Youngs sponsor a Little League team and Bob Young, with pride, points to the many trophies and awards Young's team has won.

Indeed,with all his community works, Bob Young wondered how his father found time to run his business.

Bob Young, besides being involved with supporting Little League and sponsoring a Little League team, has been a fire commissioner for fifteen years. He has been Assistant Fire Chief since he was eighteen years of age, serving under Fire Chiefs John Mataraza and Phil Martin.

At the beginning of this series the question was asked, "What does it mean to be Young at Heart?" As one can determine from all the above, being Young at heart requires being a proactive member of the community. It means caring for one's neighbors. It means being proud of one's heritage.

All too often good deeds remain unacknowledged. For your many contributions to our community and those of your family, Bob Young, thank you for being "Young at Heart".

A Family of Merritt

It seems a truism that the most interesting stories are those told by elders. Recently this writer came across what I believe to be a gem of a story. It is to be found at the library at Ulster County Community College. Written in 1903, it is told through the eyes of Nancy Rogers Merritt as recounted when she was in her eighties. The recorder was Sara A. VanDeusen Merritt, wife of Nancy Rogers Merritt's grandson. Sara had asked her when she was visiting to tell something of her young days - she was then over eighty-five years old. The following story she told while sitting close and cutting blocks for a quilt she was making for one of her granddaughters.

Nancy began her story telling of being turned out of their home by the English and then her return to New York City.

Grandmother's Story

My parents remained at Haverstraw until some time after the evacuation of the British, then they returned to New York. They found - as did many others - that their homes had either been confiscated, as ours had been, or in ashes, or in such a ruinous condition that it required the labor of months to restore them. Amid all the rejoicing over the departure of the British army, it was truly a costly victory. It was a hard struggle for my father to support his family for several years after our return to New York. Business revived slowly. But through strict economy and untiring industry, my parents once more, had as before, a comfortable little home.

My first recollection of any important event, was the inauguration of George Washington as first President of the United Sates, although I was only in my seventh year. My mother said to me on that day, several times - 'Nancy, I want you to remember this day, because New York will never see a greater one.'

My parents took me by the hand and we walked on Broadway. The streets were thronged with people. Many of them having come into the city by the common roads, by ferryboat, and by sloops and packets which had been several days in coming down the Sound on the Hudson river. Then we went to church. I particularly remember the minister saying, - 'May the blessing of heaven be upon this nations, and upon our chosen President.'

When we left the church we went to Federal Hall where the inaugural ceremony was to take place. My mother had made me a new dress for the occasion. I was particularly pleased with that, to me, beautiful homespun dress. My mother had made the waist shorter and the skirt longer than any dress I had ever had. Walking briskly along that April morning, with my parents, my new dress, the military, the music, the banners, who could have been happier than I, a little New York girl, in the year of our Lord, seventeen hundred and eighty nine!

When we were very near Federal Hall, we secured a standing place in front of a grocery store.

I was standing upon a barrel of potatoes, where my father had placed me. But as my footing was somewhat unsteady among the potatoes, my father quietly caught me up in his arms, saying: 'You can certainly see him now.' Just then I saw a man on the balcony bend low and kiss a book. Just then the bells rang, cannon boomed, bands began to play, flags were waived, and men threw their hats high in the air, and amid shouts and huzzas, cried: 'Long Live George Washington, President of the United States!' My father did not shout, neither did he throw up his hat, but I saw him draw it - slowly over his eyes, and his lips moved as if in prayer. (Is that not enough to make any patriotic heart go pitter-patter? - MLM)

Allyn Cox
Oil on Canvas

George Washington was sworn in as the nation's first president on April 30, 1789, on the balcony of Federal Hall in New York. The mural depicts (from left to right) Robert R. Livingston, chancellor of the state of New York, administering the oath; Secretary of the Senate Samuel Otis holding the Bible; George Washington, with his hand upraised; and Vice President John Adams.

Some years after, my mother told me that the day we were returning home after the inauguration, I had said to her that I was sure that George Washington would make us a bright and splendid president, because he had on such bright and splendid shoe buckles. But of saying that I have no recollection, but I do recollect that that afternoon we went to take some salt to our cows. I was particularly pleased to go out that afternoon because my mother had told me in the morning, that I could wear my new dress all day - a privilege she had never granted before. I do not think that I was a vain little girl, but one does have such a sense of freshness and cleanliness when wearing new clothes. Besides, the way my dress had been made greatly pleased me, and I wanted my friends to see it for I knew I would meet some of them on the street that afternoon.

That night we all went out to see the illumination in honor of George Washington's inauguration. The streets were a blaze of light, and every one said that the fireworks were the most beautiful New York had ever seen.

Nancy Rogers, several years later moved with her family to Marlborough. Here she met and married Morris Merritt whose family had come to Marlborough with the Purdys in 1750.

The Norton House

The year was 1941

With less than four years to go before completing a century of existence, the Richard B Norton home, located in the Mount Zion area west of here, faces ignominious demolition. The razing of this seven room frame structure will erase a landmark which has been the home of three Norton generations. The Norton property was purchased by the Town O Marlborough in August of 1930, when town officials decided to begin making provisions for a future water supply. The 45 acres which comprise the land contain 2 large springs, several small springs and a clear, fast-running brook. Town workers have already diverted the brook and piped its contents into a channel leading to the Marlboro reservoir. This move was intended to insure a high level of water to the village reservoir even in the dry summer season.

However, should this measure prove inadequate, the town could draw on its reserve supply which will be contained in two concrete spill basins on the property. These reserve tanks will be fed constantly by the two larger springs and can also be supplied with additional water by piping in the smaller springs. This preparatory work is now being done under the supervision of Water Superintendent, James Hunter.

The homestead came into the Norton family in April 1845 when James Norton of the Town of Newburgh purchased 80 acres of fertile land from James Quimby, whose descendants include Fred Quimby of Newburgh, Edward, Samuel and Harold Quimby and Mrs. James Fowler, all of Marlboro.

When James Norton died he bequeathed the property and home to his nephew, Richard B Norton. This was in May 1889. Two years later 35 acres of the land were sold to the late William C McElrath. McElrath ran a boarding house on Mountain Road. The remainder of the property remained intact until the time of Richard Norton's death in May 1930, at which time the town purchased the property.

Now 11 years later (1941) one of Marlboro's oldest houses faces destruction, along with its barns and outbuildings.

(From the Newburgh News)

The Marlborough Water Works Company was franchised in 1893. Italian immigrants furnished the labor for digging trenches and laying mains. Philip T Schantz was president. The company was sold to the Village of Marlboro in 1912. Marlboro had been an incorporated village for a few years. The incorporation for the village was dissolved in 1922. The water works were then taken over by the Town of Marlborough. The Norton property greatly enlarged the water supply for the town.

On Getting Around

The 19th century Lemon Law

If today, one goes to buy a car, one has a certain sense of security that the car will be as represented - thanks to the modern "Lemon Law". What happened when there was no such protection and one was buying not a car, but a horse?

I had an opportunity to find out when I visited the Ulster County Hall of Records recently and met with the archivist, Ken Grey. I was able to look at and photograph some of the mid 1800 County Court records. Because of the number of "locals" listed I was particularly interested in "Bingham vs Mackey". The court was hearing an appeal by William Mackey in a case that had originally been heard before Isaac Staples, JP.

Staples must have kept meticulous records as he had the testimony given, almost verbatim, from the witnesses involved.

On the first day of April last a suit was commenced before me at Marlborough, aforesaid, wherein Charles E Bingham, was plaintiff and Wm. Mackey was defendant by summons returnable on the 10th day of April at my sho (shoe) shop in Marlborough. The summons was served by Samuel H Kniffin, constable.

The plaintiff complains that some time in the year 1853 in the month of Sept., Oct. or Nov., the defendant had a public auction and then at said auction the defendant put up a bay colt, three years old, coming four in the spring, and the said colt had a bunch on his head just below his eye and the said colt was not halter broke so he could not be haltered and examined and the said defendant then and there represented that the bunch on the said colt's head had not been there but 3 or 4 days that he had seen the colt playing with some other colts a few days before that and they must have struck him then and the said plaintiff relying on the representations of said defendant bought the said colt for the sum of $69 and after the said auction sale was over the said colt was penned up and caught and the said bunch on said colt was examined and it was a hard callous lump and had been there two or three months and affected the said colt's eye and his head and rendered him of little or no value to said plaintiff whereby the said plaintiff was damaged to the amount of $50 therefore the plaintiff claims judgment for $50 and costs of suit

The case was then heard by Staples with T Bingham as attorney for Chas. E Bingham and Isaac L Craft as attorney for Wm. Mackey. Interestingly, a jury was called and chosen were Samuel L Griggs, George Maby, David Cosman, John H Baxter, Mory Wygant and James D Merritt.

Then came the testimony of the witnesses both for defense and plaintiff.

For the plaintiff were:

James Merritt - I was present at an auction of defendant last fall, ... 1853. I saw a bay colt put up at said auction that plaintiff bought - Thomas Bingham was auctioneer, the defendant said the lump had not been on said colt's head but six or eight days; the plaintiff was present at the time and said he was afraid of the lump. Defendant said they need not be afraid of it as it had not been there but 6 or 8 days. I had seen the colt and noticed the lump about six weeks previous to the sale... They could not get up to him to examine the lump, they tried to.

I was there during the sale. ... They stood alongside of the barn, David Wooley, Jeremiah Bingham, Jesse Lester, Richard Caverly and others were present at sale. I worked in the neighborhood of defendant and went acrost his field - commenced work there about six weeks previous to sale ..., saw the colt with 6 or 7 other colts in defendants fields about 1/4 of mile from defendants house.

Mory Wygant - I was present at defendant's auction sale and saw the said colt spoken of with a bunch on his face put up for sale. The defendant said the lump had not been there but a few days... The plaintiff was present and the defendant directed his conversation to him. I believe the plaintiff nor any body could get up to him to examine it. I examined it after the colt was caught after sale and found the lump hard and callous. I have doctored horses, but I never doctored anything of that kind. If the lump had not been there but six days I think it could have been cured and would have been worth more money. I think the difference would have been $20 between a hard & soft lump. I think he was sold for very near what he would have been worth without any lump. I have seen the colt lately. The lump remains about the same. ... I think the plaintiff traded the horse with Thomas Bingham. ...

Jeremiah Bingham - I have heard of this colt spoken of. I have owned him. I was present when sold. I examined the colt's head after the sale. It was callous as hard as any other part of his skull. ...I should not think it would callous in six days. ...he would not have been worth over $65 if it had not been there only of six days standing. He was not worth even $50 with it being there six weeks and callous.

Witness for the defense were -

Thomas D Bloomer - I was present at the sale spoken of ... I think I did not bid on the colt. I think he would have been worth $85 without the lump. ... It was an undersized colt

Jonathan Caverly - I was present at this sale .... I think if it had not been for the lump he would have brought $80.

Jesse W Lester - I was present at defendants sale last fall ...When the colt was put up for sale the auctioneer called the defendants attention to said colt. He said he did not know how the lump came unless the other colts had hit him a little sport.

James Q Brown - I own the horse in question and have owned him 2 or 3 weeks. This lump has not altered since I have known him. I consider him worth to me $85. I don't think it injures him for work.

David D Woolsey - I was present and clerk at the sale in question. I was present when the colt was settled for by plaintiff. ... There was no fault found by plaintiff when settled for.

Seems like the jury found for the plaintiff, Bingham, and awarded $12 damages onto which were tacked $4.94 for costs.

At the conclusion of the hearing at the higher court, Bingham again was found to have been injured and the fine assessed to Mackey was $18.98 (the original judgment plus interests) plus $13.79 for costs and disbursements for the newer trial.

The consumer triumphed!

Isaac Staples

Isaac Staples, the JP in the original case, was the son of Oliver Staples. According to Beer's Commemorative Biographical Record (1896) Oliver and his brother, David, came to Marlborough during the last decade of the 18th century. "Oliver was an itinerant shoemaker, going from house to house...He also owned a home in the village of Marlboro, and carried on a shop at that place." Sylvester in his <u>History of Ulster County</u> (1880) writes that Isaac was born in 1807 and learned the shoe trade from his father. He married Dorcas Wygant, whose father's homestead adjoined the Staples farm. His (shoe) business became so successful that he employed a number of men. He continued in the trade until 1863 when his public duties forced him to quit. He studied law and according to Sylvester, "He was careful and exact, and drew most of the legal papers required, not only for his own but for adjacent towns." In 1847 he was elected Justice of the Peace and in 1864 was sworn in as one of the justices of sessions for Ulster County.

Sorry, pictures from this era are hard to find. Here is a picture (from Sylvester) of Isaac Staples.

Over the River and Thru the Woods

It's difficult for us, familiar with highways such as 9W and the Thruway, to imagine what the roads must have been like when Marlborough was still young. There had been a number of roads laid out by the late

1700s and there were road districts and path masters and every property owner was assessed his time and labor, depending on the size of his property, to maintain the roads yearly. It was in 1807 that the State Legislature passed "An Act relative to Turnpike Companies" enabling the formation of private corporations to establish and maintain roads. It was in 1808 that Isaac Hill, amongst others, applied for and was granted a charter for the Farmers Turnpike and Bridge Company. The road was to begin at the store of James Denton in Marlborough, near the landings of Hill, Sands and Townsend, and run to the west to the Town of Shawangunk.

This is photo of map of the turnpike as registered with the County Clerk 1809

Unfortunately, the original is in poor condition

The initial investment was to be up to $5,000. The initial funds were raised by selling 600 shares at $20 each. Selah Tuthill and Thaddeus Haight were appointed the commissioners to receive the subscriptions.

Wherever possible, the original road was used, but there were some modifications that had to be made - and the property owners affected had to be reimbursed.

We whose names are hereunto subscribed and seals affixed appraisers appointed in pursuance of an application made by the President, Directors and Company of "The Farmers Turnpike and Bridge Company" to estimate and assess the damages which may be sustained by the owner or owners of lands or improvements over which the said road has been laid, having viewed the premises do estimate and assess that the several persons hereafter named have sustained the following damages by reason of said road being laid over their lands - viz.

That Amos Dickenson of the Town of Marlborough has sustained damages by reason of said road to the amount of sixty dollars

S. Adams of the Town of Marlborough by reason aforesaid has sustained damages to the amount of thirty dollars -

John Rhodes of Marlborough aforesaid has sustained damages by reason aforesaid the sum of five dollars

David Mackey of the Town of Marlborough has sustained no damage by reason aforesaid

(others given for other towns)

The Commissioners of highway for the Town of Marlborough by reason aforesaid has sustained damages to the amount of five dollars

(Deeds Liber 19 page 493)

According to the enabling act, it was lawful for the president and directors of the company to erect two gates on and across said road - one erected at a distance of not less than 3 miles from Denton's store. It is interesting to note the toll house was set almost at the boundary of the Town of Marlborough. I believe so as not to impede the usual travel on roads within the town.

This is a picture of the toll gate set up on Milton Turnpike. The building was erected c 1810

and was still standing until c 1960

Courtesy of the Mackey Family

The tolls were set:
1. For every wagon with two horses, mules or oxen, ten cents and three cents for every additional horse, mule or oxen
2. For every one horse cart, five cents

For every score of cattle, horses or mules, sixteen cents and
For every score of sheep or hog, six cents
Any person traveling said road not more than five miles west from the Hudson River was to be charged so that such persons "shall not pay more toll than is proper for the number of miles they shall travel on said turnpike."

The turnpike was completed in 1812 and was a very good road for those times. It opened the farms and lands to the west to river transportation at Milton. Grains, beef and pork, butter, sheep and wool, wood, hay and other products were carted to Milton and shipped from the docks there. According to Woolsey, "It added great prosperity to the Milton part of town for thirty years or more…Lumber, building supplies and iron for blacksmith work were sold here. There were tailors, hatters, cabinet makers and artisans of all kinds; there were soap works, sash and blind factory and a paper was printed. Milton saw its greatest prosperity."

The stock in the Farmers Turnpike Company proved to be quite valuable as witnessed by the Will of Henry Crawford (date March 27, 1816).

"To my nephew Henry Crawford son of Daniel Crawford and Nelly Crawford $300" "and my $200 in the Farmers turnpike stock."

The charter of the Farmers Turnpike Company was amended in 1818 and the toll fees were reduced. The amendment also provided for special consideration for people, "passing thru said gate for worship or a funeral or a grist mill for the grinding of grain for his family use, or a blacksmith's shop to which he usually resorts for work to be done or attending court when legally summoned as a juror or witness or a militia training, or a town meeting or election at which he is entitled to vote, or going for a physician or midwife … or from his common business on his farm,"

This, however, was not enough to satisfy John Young. In 1853 he refused to pay the toll and was brought to court. He lost, but continued by appealing the case. Apparently he was questioning the Company's right to erect a toll gate. The answering attorney replied:

It was urged on the argument by the appellants' attorney that the plaintiffs should have shown on the trial that they had a license from the Governor of the State to erect the gates...This right was given by the charter, and the road was built and the gates erected pursuant to the Charter. Although it is unnecessary to argue it, I think it beyond question, if the Charter had contained no such provision, the facts that the gates had been erected for thirty years, that during that period toll had been taken at them would raise the legal presumption that the gates were lawfully there.

The toll house was sold in 1857 to Isaac Craft who turned right around and sold it to Jacob Handley. In 1883 the property was owned by Thorn Mackey and remained in the Mackey family. It was torn down c 1960.

Again reporting on the Turnpike, Woolsey writes:

"The very old people along the route of the road will well remember the large amount of trouble over it. There was said to be twenty taverns along the road for the use and convenience of the men and teams, mostly the men, who could obtain their meals for a trifle and the best of rums and whiskeys at three cents a glass."

Near the other end of the Farmers Turnpike in Milton stood the Crowell house. About the year 1967 this picture was taken of the house.

Crowell house c 1967

In a brief write-up Liz Plank wrote:

Only a few years ago this former hotel was restorable but has since fallen apart. In the twenties a lady of Modena or Wallkill, then in her eighties, told this reporter, Mrs. Plank, that when she was 8, 9, 10, and 11, she went every year with her grandparents on a wagon or walking, and an ox team, to the Milton dock with honey to sell along the way and at Milton. They camped along the Turnpike, which was their route, but stayed a few days at this house. Every night families sang together and children loved to go.

One of the Crook families once lived here and had a blacksmith shop here. In the twenties owned and occupied by Grace Crowell Hewitt and her nephew, Ralph Crowell, of the Central Hudson Steamship lines.

When the West Shore was being built in the '80s (i.e. 1880s) workmen roomed and boarded here with the Crooks.

Fortunately, there came along people with a vision of what could be and transformed the "falling apart" building into a warm and cozy home.

The Milton Turnpike, as a "modern" road is now well over 100 years old. It has been and still remains a major artery into the heartland of Marlborough.

Celebrating the River, the People and the Land

On Nov 6, 2005 the Marlboro Yacht Club hosted a CELEBRATION. They celebrated 50 years of incorporation and 10 years in their new club house, of which they are very proud.

Things are relatively quiet at the club house now, the boats are all lined neatly on their winter perches. During the summer, boating season it is a hub of activity. It is indeed pleasurable to sit on the front porch, listen to the call of the birds and the soft lapping of the river as it kisses the shore, and let one's eyes wander over the lovely boats that lie tied to their moorings - each with its own colors, each with its own charm. One can watch the activity on the river which, during the summer, is extensive - tugs, barges, oil tankers, graceful sail boats, motor boats of all sizes - as they ply their way up or down the river. One sees and hears the railroad train across the river as it winds its way up or down from New York City to Albany or beyond. Closer at hand, one sees, hears and feels the rush of the West Shore Railroad as it too wends its way laden with freight cars of every description.

The land on which the Yacht Club stands has long been in service to the community. Early on it belonged to Lewis DuBois and how many ships landed at his dock can only be guessed. It is believed that there was a steam ferry operating from the dock to Hampton and New Hamburg on the other side of the river. In 1856 the land was sold to William C Young. He expanded on the dock that was there. It is supposed the "Queen of Wappingers Falls" was the first boat to land at this dock.

JAMES W. BALDWIN 1861
renamed CENTRAL HUDSON 1903

Built at Jersey City, N. J., wood, 925 tons, by M. S. Allison for Capt. Jacob H. Tremper as night boat for route between New York and Rond-out. Sold to Central Hudson Steamboat Co. in 1899 and renamed central hudson in 1903. Dismantled in 1912.

An article in the <u>New Paltz Independent</u>, April 10, 1873 indicated:

The people of Marlborough should feel under considerable obligation to Mr. William Young for getting the splendid steamers "Baldwin" and "Cornell" to stop at his dock. Besides the great expense of building the docks, he has spent over one thousand dollars in making a road where it is a credit to him and a great benefit to the public. He has done more for the profit of the people of Marlborough for the last two years than any other person in the town.

In 1884 he brought his son, Charles, into partnership as WC Young & Son. The "Upper Dock" became a very busy place. Charles had children Ralph P., William C. and Adelaide T. who married Louis B Traphagen.

In an interview several years ago John Lynn spoke of the activity at Young's dock. The "fruit" boats played a most important role in Marlborough's history. John remembers when the farmers' laden, horse drawn wagons would be parked from the dock clear up Dock Road and onto 9W. The "Poughkeepsie", the "O'Dell", the "Homer Ramsdel" and the "Jacob Trumper" were mostly all fruit boats. John says he can remember a day when the "Poughkeepsie" was loading fruit at the dock and the "Jacob Trumper" was treading water in the river waiting to pull in. There was a cherry pitting factory down at the docks. It was a small operation which would wash and pit the cherries and add sugar to them. The cherries were used to make pies down in New York City. There was also a rather long building near the present Yacht club. Local farmers would rent space in the building from Ralph Young to store their fruit for short periods of time. John said the poles holding the building erect had the names of the farmers who were renting those spaces. The building stood until recent years. There was also a weigh station. Large barn doors at one end allowed a horse and wagon or truck to enter. The scale where the fruit was weighed, right on the vehicle, was in the center of the building. Barn doors at the opposite end of the building permitted the vehicle to exit while another vehicle could then enter through the first doors. John Hedeman was the last to live in the old "weigh station" on the Yacht Club property. He built a boat in the long building.

Weigh Station at Yacht Club

With the growth of shipping fruit via trucks, the call for river boat transportation fell drastically. For a number of years, the dock was virtually inactive. Plank (<u>History of the Town of Marlborough</u>) wrote "Where now are only rotted timers, the Young dock reached out over the river until recent years and until the twenties was a busy place when the steamers came in."

John Lynn was instrumental in founding the Marlborough Yacht Club. Some of the original members included Fran Johnson, Jim Paltridge, Christie Tuttle, John Manion, Harry Lyons and Cluett Schantz. A Yacht Club pamplet also lists Len Schreiber, Carl Rodes, Harry Limes, Charles Dayton, Alton Sarles, Mike Catila and DeWitt Quick with other early members listed as Frank DeGeorge, Sam Quimby and Bard Presler. They were able to purchase the Traphagen/Young property of about four acres at the Marlboro dock in the early 1940s. John served as Commodore from 1950 to 1955. Dick and Flo Barcia ran the small restaurant down at the Yacht Club for a number of years giving nonmembers an opportunity to partake of the ambiance of the Marlboro River front.

In 1948 the Marlboro Yacht Club played a significant part in the worldwide event, the Out Board Motor Races from Albany to New York City. The Marlboro club was the only gas stop. In the early 1950s the club held Out Board Motor Races that attracted many spectators, as many as two or three thousand people. .

Signing the papers Feb 10, 1955 for the incorporation of the Marlboro Yacht Club were Charles W Brown, Joseph Marchione, John P Lynn, Bard R Presler, Vincent G Fowler and Ira Merwin. The directors chosen, until a yearly meeting could be held, were: Charles W Brown, Marlboro; Ira Merwin, Wallkill; Joseph Marchione, Newburgh; Francis J Johnson, Marlboro and Edmond P Sarles, Marlborough.

Club House & Resturant
May 20, 1969

Past Commodores of the Marlboro Yacht Club include: 1941-1949 Harry Lyons, Sr., Francis Johnson, and Esmond Sarles; 1950 to 1955 John Lynn; 1956-1959 John Ronk; 1960-1961 Merwyn Maharay; 1962-1963 Harry Lyons; 1964-1967 Oliver Cosman; 1968-1970 Thomas Hickey; 1971 John Ronk; 1972-1974 Joe Primavera; 1975 John Ronk; 1976-1977 Sam Quimby; 1978-1979 John Bull; 1980 William Holik; 1981 John Bull; 1982 Dale Newhart; 1983 John Milici; 1984 Joe Primavera; 1985-1986 John Bull; 1987-1988 Herb Silcocx; 1989-1990 Paul Baymore; 1991 Ron Colandrea; 1992-1994 Sam Quimby; 1995 Bill Fox; 1996-2001 Ron Tomlins; 2002-2003 George Carl. The present Commodore is Neal Wyckoff.

Marlboro Yacht Club 2005

Skating on the Hudson

Marlborough is fortunate to be located on the banks of one of the most beautiful rivers in the world! Since primeval days the Hudson has played a significant part in our history. The first sighting of what was to become Marlborough was made from the deck of Henry Hudson's boat; many of our early settlers came by water; ferries and docks led to early prosperity for the town, shad and other fishing on the Hudson has added romance to our story; and many of Marlborough's early industries were located close to the river.

Whenever I cross the Hudson River I ask my grandsons, "Don't you think my Hudson River is beautiful?" They chide me for calling it "my" Hudson River. I then tell them of the lesson I learned more than fifty years ago in Paul Georgini's English class. He had had us read, "Who Owns the Mountains" in which the author explains that whoever loves the mountains owns them. I tell my grandsons, if they love the Hudson, then they, too, own the Hudson.

I was particularly stricken with a book recently read at the Crawford House in Newburgh. Entitled, "The Hudson Highlands" the book was written by William Howell and published posthumously in 1933. He writes of his early experiences:

I was born and raised on the Hudson River, on Newburgh Bay,

where ice skating in America may be said to have taken its rise. When I was half grown the Donoghues of Newburgh were in their prime, Joseph F Donaghue being the champion amateur skater of the world in all distances from the sprints to a hundred miles. It was natural that the boys thereabouts would take to skating, and whenever a Donoghue or other speed skater appeared on the river, some of us would get behind him and follow his stride as long as we were able to keep up.

He goes on to explain how he and his friends made their own skates. He called them "straights" where the blades were 16, 18 or even 20 inches long. He had a pair made from car springs with the wood made from an old apple tree which had been cured two years before using. He reports, "Apple wood combines strength and lightness".

Perhaps the thing I found most fascinating with his story was the distance one could skate back then. He reports that he could make 15 to 20 miles an hour without fatigue and he had skated from Newburgh to West Point, 9 miles, in half an hour and to Poughkeepsie, 16 miles, in an hour. According to Howell, one could skate all the way from Yonkers to Troy. Interestingly, he reports that an automobile went on the ice on the Hudson for the first time in 1906.

Closer to our time, several neighbors reported on their experiences skating on the Hudson. George Greiner skated from Marlboro to Milton to court his future wife. It must have been worth the trip as the marriage lasted sixty years!

Carol Felter reported being surprised to find out her mother, Ernestine, was a good skater. She recalls skating from near the Marlboro dock and seeing a lot of people on the ice. Some sections were very smooth, but some were quite rough. She was struck by the fact that the ice cutter couldn't make it up the river.

Cynthia Carpenter Gervais called from California to report on her skating experiences. She was little at the time and also skated from near the dock. She remembers the skates being strapped to her feet. She went with her mother and father. Her father, Ed Carpenter, was manager of the Marlboro Bank for many years. Cynthia reports her mother brought a Windsor chair that she pushed on ahead of herself. "She wasn't about to fall and break anything."

The last time Bruno Ronkese remembers skating on the Hudson was circa 1944. Bruno said, "The Hudson was our playground" - swimming, row boating, fishing and skating were the primary sports with some trapping thrown in. He remembers the "racer" skates - Johnson skates had a star cut out of the bottom where the blade meets the shoe. Hockey skates were "sissy" skates. He loved his skates even though, according to him, he could only make right turns - he never could manage left.

That didn't stop him, though. He and his brother, Al, and Willie and Joe DeFabio would skate across the Hudson to New Hamburg. He continued, "Skating was never done alone, the ice had cracks and it was too dangerous."

The newspaper in New Hamburg would publish their names as the first "from across the frozen river visitors of the season". They would go and flirt with the New Hamburg girls. He tells of the time he and the other boys pushed a horse sleigh across the river to New Hamburg - they would push the girls around in the sleigh, the New Hamburg boys got jealous, stole the sleigh and sank it.

Bruno went to school at the Cedar Cliff one room school house. He remembers his teacher, Mrs. Russell B Kohl, taking him and a few other kids to NFA. They had the opportunity of shaking hands

Bruno Ronkese owns the Hudson River

with Admiral Byrd. Bruno reports his recollection of Byrd circa 1936 was that Byrd had a "raspy" voice.

The river ice skating season was not long as "it takes awhile for the river to cool down" and the Hudson does contain some salt at this point. They often would wait for the ice cutter to go upriver and then would jump across the cut. The best laid plans....one time they were in New Hamburg and the ice cutter came through and they couldn't get back home.

It would seem the river doesn't belong to me alone. Each of the above, in recalling their experiences of years ago, exposed a great love for the river and the memories it evokes. I guess it is true that whoever really loves the river owns it.

Do you own the Hudson?

Many thanks to those who contributed to this story - I appreciate your willingness to share.

Ferries Across the Hudson

In 1866 Benson J Lossing wrote a book entitled, "The Hudson from The Wilderness to the Sea". He peppered the book with many interesting photos and observations.

"A pleasant glimpse of Marlborough, through a broad ravine, may be obtained from the rough eminence above the New Hamburg tunnel, and also from the lime-kilns at the foot of the bluff, at the edge of the river, where a ferry connects the two villages." He has included a picture of Marlborough from the lime kilns in New Hamburg.

Lossing gives some of the history of ferries on the Hudson. He writes, "The first horse boat powered by a team of horses, the ferry, 'Moses Roger', was launched in Newburgh on July 16, 1816, and used on the crossing until she was replaced by steam in 1828". He describes it as a flat-bottomed craft with a wheel in the center. The first crossing of the "Moses Roger" was Aug. 10, 1816. It's astonishing to learn it carried, "a coach and horses, a wagon and horse, 17 chaises and horses, a lone horse and 50 passengers".

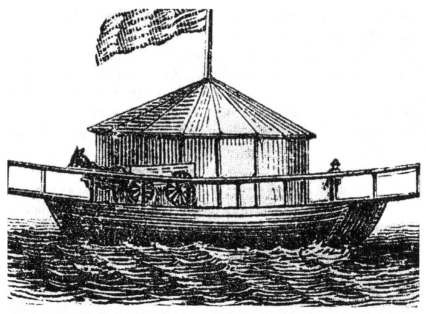

the Moses Roger - July 16, 1816

Lossing also writes about Marlborough and Milton indicating, "Opposite Spring Brook is the village of Milton, remarkable, like its sister, Marlborough, a few miles below for the picturesque beauty of the surrounding country and the abundance of Antwerp raspberries produced in its vicinity every year. There and at some places on the eastern shore, are the chief sources of the supply of that delicious fruit for the city of New York, and the quantity raised is so great, that a small steamboat is employed for the sole purpose of carrying raspberries daily to the city. These villages are upon high banks, and are scarcely visible from the river. They have a background of rich farming lands, terminating beyond a sweet valley by a range of lofty hills that are covered with the primeval forest. They are the resort of New Yorkers during the heat of summer".

Milton Ferry and horse boat

Lossing also has a picture of the Milton Ferry and Horse Boat. Again, the year being 1866 he writes, "The boat was keeping alive the memory of times before steam was used for navigation. It was one of only two vessels of the kind upon the Hudson in 1860, that were propelled by horse power. The other was at Coxsakie. The Milton ferryboat has since been withdrawn (1866)".

In 1872 Wm. Nicklin wrote a letter to his parents who were due to come to Marlboro shortly. He gives a good glimpse into the life of a small farmer in Marlboro at the time:

Marlboro Ulster Co NY
Sunday Sept. 29 (1872)

Dear Father and Mother:

(Here he gives news of how the family and farm are going.
He then continues to give them directions about how to get to Marlboro. Note he mentions the ferry from New Hamburg.)

I think you had better, instead of getting off railroad train at Poughkeepsie, go to next station, New Hamburg - 7 miles nearer and nearly opposite Marlboro landing on the west side of the river. Ask anyone for the ferryman or mailman, John Harbison. He will row you over. He will tell Millard Bros. (at the) Marlboro dock, to get your freight and bring it over in their boat to Marlboro. Then I can get a horse and haul it up for you. I tell you this in case I should accidentally miss you which is unlikely if you name the day you will be on hand here. Don't forget the alteration of place of getting off, the river will surely be open (no ice-skating on the river yet) and you get off train some nearer to us. Don't confound Newburgh, 7 miles south of us and reached by Erie RR, with New Hamburg; opposite Marlboro 7 miles below Poughkeepsie on the Hudson River RR. I will close up having to shave, wash etc.

Love to both.
Affectionately,
William

PS Had any frost yet up your way? None here yet but the leaves are leaving the trees. I send you this week's paper - I vote for Greeley.

I can remember as a kid, coming to Marlboro by crossing the Hudson via the Newburgh Beacon ferry. It was always a highlight of the trip as we were able to get out of the car, watch one shore fade into the distance while seeing the opposite shore approach. And there was always the clanging of bells as they tied the dock ropes and signaled to the drivers to begin their exit from the ferry.

I was working in Newburgh during the 1960s and 70s when the Newburgh-Beacon ferry made its last voyage - the bridge had opened a short time before. Dr. Harold Monson was the long time Superintendent of Schools at the time and a most enlightened educator. Dr. Monson had the foresight to have all of the Newburgh School District students take a ride on the ferry before it closed. There are a good many locals now who remember riding on that ferry.

Progress? There is now word that the new Newburgh-Beacon ferry will be up and running shortly (NB it is). Anyone who has had to fight the Beacon hill in order to park for the train to NYC or wherever, will welcome the news as will anyone who nostalgically looks back to the times when there were ferries across the Hudson.

Buckley's Bridge

Several weeks ago there was a request for information about Buckley's Bridge - how old was it? when was it built? when is the last time it was repaired? Unfortunately, I didn't have the answers to the questions, thus had to do some searching.

Buckley's Bridge circa 1915

Buckley's Bridge is located in the Kennedy Patent - a 2000 acre grant from King George 1 to Archibald Kennedy. King George was known as the "German" king as he was born and raised in Hanover, Germany and had lived there until he was 54 years old and was crowned king of England. ("George, by the Grace of God, King of Great Britain, France and Ireland, Defender of the Faith, etc.") He was not a fluent speaker of the English language but spoke his native German even while inhabiting the British royal palace.

The Patent was actually in two pieces. One piece was 1200 acres on the south east border of our town - it extended from Bloom Street down to the county line. It would seem that Archibald Kennedy was actually buying the land for Lewis Gomez (of Gomez Mill House), as Gomez was not a British citizen and thus could not obtain a Patent. Lewis Gomez got his Denizen papers and in 1716 bought the land from Archibald Kennedy. Lewis Gomez died and in 1748 his sons, Mordecai

101

and David sold the full 1200 acres to William Campbell and Archibald Duffie. In 1750 Campbell and Duffie sold the land to George Merritt and Francis Purdy who were both from Westchester County. One of my last stories spoke of a descendent of George Merritt.

In 1751 Merritt and Purdy agreed to split the land almost in exact halves. Here comes the interesting part. The agreement to split the land describes the division line:

Agreed by and between the said Francis Purdy and George Merrit that the creek or run of water commonly called and known by the name of the saw mill creek (we presently call it "Jew's Creek") from where the highway crosses said creek shall be the partition or division of that part of the herein before described tract lying between said highway and Hudson's River - the benefit of the stream from said highway to said river to be and remain in common and that a line of marked trees running west from a stone set up on the west side of said highway at the distance of 2 chains and 2 rods measured on a straight line N from a bridge laid over said saw mill creek shall be the division

Thus it would seem that in 1751 there already existed a bridge over the stream.

How did the bridge get it's popular name? It was named after John Buckley who had a large home nearby. John Buckley was the son of John Buckley who was born in Stuttgart, Germany in 1755 and was trained as a carpenter. He came to America in 1776 as a soldier fighting with General Burgoyne at Saratoga. He became a prisoner and spent some time in prison in Boston. His son, John was born in 1786 and learned the carpenter's trade from his father. He later went to Providence where he worked as a millwright and machinist. He worked with Samuel Slater who was called the father of American manufacturing. Thereafter he worked in Dutchess and Orange county bring his expertise to this area. During the War of 1812, imports of cotton goods hit bottom and thus there was a demand for domestic products. The manufacturing of cotton goods thrived. In 1815 Buckley decided he wanted to venture out on his own.

He bought a carding and spinning mill located on Old Man's Creek that had been established several years before. He did carding and spinning for farmers in Ulster and Orange County. This was in a period before the large fruit farms as are presently in Marlborough and there were many sheep growers. Since much of the clothing used in that period was homemade, Buckley did well by taking over the onerous task of carding and spinning the wool which the women of the area could then weave into cloth for clothing. His mill became known as the Marlborough Woolen Factory. Buckley developed a wide reputation for quality products and won awards for the best blue broadcloth made from American wool.

In 1877 the Caywoods bought a piece of property bordering on Buckley's Bridge. They later established "Shady Brook Farm", a boarding house. In the early 1920's one of the frequent guests was Alfred Maurer. Maurer, born in 1868, was the son of Louis, a highly successful graphic artist for Currier and Ives. He spent his early adult years in Paris studying art. He knew and was a guest at times of Gertrude Stein and her circle. He returned to the US just before the outbreak of WW1. Alfred Maurer was known as the "Father of Modernism" in American painting. It has been reported he was "artistically light years ahead" of his time. He has had a loyal following ever since. He painted a number of works while in Marlboro including one of Buckley's Bridge.

Mildred Marconic reported her early memories as she lived down the Old Post Road in the middle of Buckley's Hill opposite the Shady Brook Farm. Old Post Road was the old Rt. 9W at that time. She remembered the boarding house at Shady Brook Farm as a place where there was always activity and interesting people.

Shady Brook Farm later passed into the hands of Lou and Edith Meckes. Edith was born a Caywood. Their daughter, Margaret Meckes Conroy, wrote a number of years ago, of her remembrances of her parents' business. The main house had 8 bedrooms for boarders and cottages with eight bedrooms apiece. They could accommodate nearly 50 people at one time. Boarders enjoyed having the leisure to go swimming, (there is a dam right near Buckley's Bridge that provides for a deeper pool of water), play tennis (they had clay courts), croquet, and enjoy the sociability of other guests, the good meals and the countryside. In the evenings some of the boarders would walk to Marlboro to go to the movies or to have ice cream at "Fromell's".

No need to remind people of the fact that Buckley's Bridge has been closed for a period of time, but funding has come through for the necessary repairs. Gael Appler said "Buckley's Bridge is a masterpiece of stone construction - it has pretty intricate stone work - wingwalls made up of laid up stone and a laid up stone arch".

Indeed, the very image of the bridge conjures up the realization that Buckley's Bridge is indeed a bridge from Marlborough's past to a yet unknown future.

The Milton RailRoad Station

The Milton Railroad Station is significant as it is a remaining landmark of an era important to the Hudson River Valley. Architecturally it is a well preserved example of a nineteenth century railroad passenger/freight station. The railroad has played a significant part in the history both of Milton and indeed of the entire United States. It is likened to arteries that carry the lifeblood (raw materials and manufactured products, people) to every part of the body corporate. The site of the railroad station carries a fascinating story of man's struggle into the twenty-first century.

Since the site is one where the terrain is flat at the river's edge, allowing for easy entrance and exit from the river, it was used as such by the Native Americans long before the European settlers arrived. There is evidence of a Native American burial ground a short distance away

The town of Marlborough remained unsettled by Europeans until 1709.

In 1709 Queen Anne granted a patent to George Barbarie for 2,000 acres in the northeast portion of the town. In 1710 Captain William Bond was granted a patent for 600 acres to the immediate south of the Barbarie patent. The site of the train station straddles the Bond and the Barbarie Patents.

Abner Brusch, who owned the south half of the Barbarie Patent, where Milton now is, or his grantor, Richard Albertson, built a log house at the Conklin place, Milton, about 1740. In 1776 Brusch lost the land and it fell into the hands of Samuel Hallock, a quaker. In 1786 Hallock's widow turned the property over to Benjamin Sands. Either Hallock or Sands built a dock with supporting buildings at the site. In a deed from 1799 from Benjamin Sands to Isaac Hill it says "Beginning at a rock marked 'IH' to Sutton's line or north bounds of

Bond's patent, along said patent line to road leading from Sutton's saw mill to the river - dwelling house, store house and wharf".

Thus we can see there was already, in 1799, a dock and other buildings on the property. This area is where first sail, and then steamships picked up and dropped off cargoes and passengers. Several boats were constructed in the vicinity. Milton became a bustling port on the river in the mid 1800s. The famous "Mary Powell" had a stop at Milton.

Because of the ability to utilize the river in such a convenient way, the area around the dock blossomed and grew. In 1808 the Farmer's Bridge and Turnpike Company was established with none other than the aforementioned Isaac Hill as a prime mover. The turnpike opened up the more western areas and goods and produce were carried along the Turnpike to the dock. Warehouses lined the waterfront and factories and commercial facilities were established also.

A wheelbarrow factory was started. New and larger buildings were constructed near what became the West Shore station in Milton. The New York Gazetteer published in 1860 says that the plant was turning out 40,000 wheelbarrows a year at that time . In another article it is written that the factory burned in 1869 but was rebuilt. Sylvester reports the new factory as being 46 by 70 feet, with a wing 28 by 70 feet and three stories high. Both steam and water power were employed in the building. Sylvester put the value of the plant at $10,000 and another $10,000 for the equipment and machinery utilized. In 1885 H.H. Bell & sons bought the property and operated a plush factory there altering the building to suit their needs. Again the building was enlarged. The building became a four story structure with 17,000 square feet of floor space. The Bells originally had a plush and glove lining plant. From the size of the building it is obvious they were doing quite well. This became one of the chief businesses in the town.

It was during this time that the railroad station was built in Milton adjacent to the Bell's factory. The railroad took advantage of the importance of that area to the community at large. It was the hub of the commercial center of the area at that time. According to statistics, the town of Marlborough grew from a small community of 2,733 in 1865 to a thriving village of 3,978 by 1900. Adjacent to the docks were taverns, stores, supplies and hotels. (See map Beers 1875)

People of Marlborough met the potential of a rail line through their town with mixed emotions as it was a two edged sword. While the railroad would greatly ease transportation and bring commerce to the town, it also came between the town and the river.

Jacob Handley already had a flourishing business (or businesses) at the site and was a major player in the attempt to stop the railroad. For many years he has was the leading owner of real estate in the town, and was credited with doing a lot in building up and beautifying the village. He was the owner of both the hotels in Milton. As a member of the firm of Pratt, Handley & Co., he engaged largely in the transportation business on the Hudson at one time, and subsequently carried on that business for several years himself. He owned the principal dock at Milton.

There were numerous suits between the railroad and local landowners. It was in 1882 that several of those holding out lost the case and were forced into selling their riverside property to the railroad.

The first trains to travel the west shore of the Hudson belonged to the West Shore Railway. The first passenger train left Kingston for New York City on the morning of June 25, 1883. That it was an important occasion is evidenced by the fact that in Kingston incoming trains were met by bands of music and ringing of bells. The West Shore railroad was considered by many to be a great benefit to the community. "It furnishes refrigerator cars and ships fruit wherever desired. The great hotels of New York City, Philadelphia, Boston, Montreal and others cities are furnished with peaches and other fruit direct from here".

While in the early nineteenth century, the river was a primary form of transportation, with the startup of the railroad, that began to change. John Matthews, former Town of Marlborough Historian writes: "The 'Horse and Buggy Days' for the Town of Marlborough ended in the early 1920's." About that time Walter McMichaels reopened Bell's Factory, under the name of the Milton Woolen Mills. In the late 1920's another plant was built adjacent to the Bell's factory and operated as the Institutional Supply Co.

Shortly thereafter, the big four-story frame structure used by the Bells was razed to make room for a larger concrete block cold storage facility. Since the primary product of the area is fruit, it is understandable that cold storage plants became a vital link in the fruit production business. The building site, right next to the railroad station, and so near the Milton dock, eased the transition from tree to table.

The railroad was a vital part of the community. There were a number of boarding houses springing up and several advertised they were close to the Milton railroad station and thus could be easily reached by train. Locals would take the train to neighboring cities to take care of necessary business. Marlborough Schools were not yet accredited to confer a high school diploma. School students wishing to graduated from an accredited high school traveled to Newburgh to attend the high school there. A major means of transportation was the railroad. Various members of the community have reported going to the movies in Newburgh by train.

Note, the dock was still functioning. Some older members of the Milton community recall that there was a drug store south of the library that also had an ice cream counter. This was quite the convening spot, especially during the summer. Many of the local guesthouse owners would meet and pick up the tourist there, just after the tourists had alighted from the Day Boat at the dock. Mike Canosa, former supervisor of the Town of Marlborough, recalled the steamship Mary Powell and the role she played in Milton's history. "We were a river town" he said.

However, transportation by boat gave way as transportation by train became easier and more available.

Mike Canosa shared some of his memories of the railroad. When he was scheduled to report for military duty for W.W.II, his father brought him to the Milton Railroad station to catch the train. When Canosa finished his duties, he also arrived back in Milton by railroad. Thus it can be seen, the railroad station was the scene of both heart wrenching and heart warming family events.

The site of the railroad station was indeed busy and a focal point for the community. One can only guess at how many people traveled through this station. The station was an attractive building and similar to many that dotted the tracks of the railroad.

Alas, transportation by train began to wane as more and more trucking firms began transporting fruit and people were able to afford automobiles. The Railroad ceased passenger service in 1959.

The Railroad company sold an unused portion of their land which included the train station in 1963 to George Hildebrand. The acreage of that site being .81A. In 1968 the land and buildings were sold to Herman Herzog. Herzog sold to Royal Kedem Winery which for a period of time ran an operation at the old Bell's factory and at the old railroad station. The railroad station was used as a wine tasting room and while some changes were made, attempts were made to keep the ambiance of a small rural train station.

The Winery donated the land and the buildings thereon to the Town of Marlborough in 1998.

Current Status

All the commercial and industrial operations are now gone except for the west shore railroad line which is still present and active although only for freight. The Milton Railroad Station site presently contains one building that holds the distinction of being included on the National Register, the historic train station terminal.

The Milton Railroad Station is an excellent example of the architecture used by railroads for small community depots. Many of its features can be considered charming as well as historical. The fact that so little change has been made in the station over a period of over 100 years bears testament to the attraction of the building design as well as the quality of workmanship that went into the building. It's history conjures up a significant part in the history of the Town of Marlborough. Its being holds the potential to give the interpretation of that history to future generations.

Glen Clarke At Milton Railroad Station

An interesting, I think, aside:

During the era of the building of the West Shore Railroad there were a great many mergers of smaller lines into what later became seven or eight large railroad empires covering the United States. Each of these was presided over by its respective "Robber Baron". One of the corrupt competitive practices of the time, was the setting up of parallel railroad lines. One "Baron" would purposely invade another's territory and set up a competitive railroad and then start a rate war based on cut throat practices.

The Pennsylvania RailRoad invaded the territory of the New York Central which was then headed by William H. Vanderbilt. The West Shore was chartered in 1881 to build a line on the west side of the Hudson paralleling Vanderbilt's property all the way to Buffalo.

The original West Shore started at Jersey City with stations at Hoboken and Weehawken before continuing north. By the end of 1883, it was running all the way through to Buffalo. Naturally, Vanderbilt retaliated. He started to build the South Pennsylvania

RailRoad purposely to parallel the Pennsylvania RailRoad's main line between Philadelphia and Pittsburgh. To show how nasty the situation got, the West Shore received financial aid from George M. Pullman who hated Vanderbilt. Vanderbilt, it seems, would not use Pullman sleeping cars on his line. He used Wagner Palace Cars instead.

Vanderbilt, on the other hand, was aided in his South Pennsylvania RailRoad endeavor by Andrew Carnegie who did not like the Pennsylvania's RailRoad's monopoly in Pittsburgh. The competition between the West Shore and Vanderbilt's New York Central caused the West Shore to flounder first. It went bankrupt in June 1884. However the financial damage the West Shore was doing to the New York Central alarmed J.P. Morgan, a friend of Vanderbilt's. Morgan decided to intervene.

In July 1885 Morgan invited Roberts of the Pennsylvania and Vanderbilt of the Central to a meeting on his palatial yacht to try and arrange a truce while slowly cruising the East River and Long Island Sound. Morgan succeeded and in return for control of the bankrupt West Shore, Vanderbilt agreed to stop any further construction on the South Pennsylvania RailRoad.

It is believed that J.P. Morgan received fees estimated at between one and three million for arranging this "deal" between Roberts and Vanderbilt. New York Central kept the name "West Shore" on its stock, tickets and timetables for years.

(from Ken Kinlock <k_kinlock@yaloo.com>)

Of Work

Tools of the Trade

Ever wonder what equipment an old fashioned blacksmith had in order to perform his arduous work? In 1789 Latting Carpenter, yeoman from New Marlborough (actually lived in Lattingtown) sold his tools to John Carpenter, blacksmith, New Marlborough, for £14 - current lawful money of the state of New York.

He sold, "One set of Blacksmith's tools namely one pair of bellows, one anvil, one vice, one sledge, three hand hammers and five pair of tongs and also one set of nailing tools namely one bellows, four stakes and 2 hammers". I would assume the nailing tools were used in the shoeing of horses.

At that point in Marlborough's history, Lattingtown was quite a hub of activity, and, naturally had at least one blacksmith shop. Does this not conjure up the image of, "under the spreading chestnut tree..."

And, yes, at that time it was "Lattingtown" named after the Lattingtown that the Latting family had left on Long Island when they came to Marlborough. I don't know just when the "g" got dropped and it became "Lattintown".

A Wayfaring Man

Recently, while doing research at Crawford House - home of the Historical Society of Newburgh Bay and the Highlands, I came across a most interesting book - Hines Annual - the West Bank of the Hudson River - Albany to Tappan - written by CG Hines in 1906. This book, one of only 52 copies made is most interesting in that it had pictures pasted into it by the author. Each copy had different pictures, thus each copy was truly unique. I considered it quite a find, as there were originally only 52 copies and they are almost 100 years old.

Hines captions the book by writing, "Notes on its history and legends, its ghost stories and romances, gathered by a wayfaring man who may now and then have error therein - CG Hines."

About Marlboro he writes:

Old Man's Creek and Major Lewis DuBois are so inseparably connected that to speak of one is to mention the other. The hill which modestly poses here at the river bank (we are in Marlboro) affords the creek an opportunity for some grand lofty tumbling before it reaches the lower level. The series of beautiful falls and rapids thus formed were early turned to account by the Major, whose mill is an ancient landmark. In fact he had three mills here at different levels; two of them are today in operation. The grist mill still using the overshot wheel. This is a beautiful little picture spot. Towards the river one sees the old mill, with the wooden waterway and a bit of the wheel, while beyond through the branches of the leafless trees is to be seen the single stone arch of the wagon bridge and still further unlimited space.

(NB this "wagon bridge" is today's bridge under 9W)

The Lewis DuBois Mill on Old Man's Creek - Marlboro.

From Hines book

(I apologize for the poor quality of the photo - remember it is almost 100 years old).

Looking up stream, the eye follows the plank sluice to the dam through whose curtain of Crystal water can be seen the moss covered rock of its construction. At the left a great boulder juts out, which affords the water a fine opportunity for display, while beyond all this tumble and hubbub is the hush of the mill pond with its fringe of autumn foliage, a sight to tempt the painter's brush.

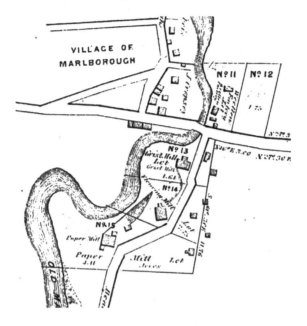

1841 Parmeter Map

Doing research at the City of Newburgh Records Management Office, I was able to get (courtesy of Betsy McKean) an 1841 map done of the Lewis DuBois property which included the various mill lots. This map was done by Stephen C Parmenter, Surveyor. Parmenter left quite a legacy as his maps have long been noted for their accuracy and detail.

Will Plank, almost 50 years after Hines, also wrote about the DuBois Mills. Plank writes:

"Resigning from the army in 1779 DuBois spent most of his time looking after his many interests in Marlborough. He had a grain mill on the dock road near the cataract of Old Man's Creek and furnished wheat to the Continental army at West Point. Later he established a fulling mill and woolen factory at the smaller falls later used by Woolsey Wright's grist mill back of the present site of the Marlborough mill. ...DuBois died in 1802 and his son Lewis carried on his milling business...."

While Woolsey mentions the DuBois Mill, Cochrane writing in 1887 does a good job of giving the chronology of the mill. Cochrane mentions that grist mills and saw mills were the first manufacturing industries carried on in Marlborough. He writes, Lewis DuBois "held all the land about the vicinity of Old Man's Creek and the river flats in front, together with all the water privileges in the southern part of town. He was largely interested in the milling business... He also owned and operated the woolen factory, now operated by Woolsey Wright as a grist mill."

The DuBois Mill-pond,
From Hines book

According to Cochrane the mill was built about 1806. In 1826 David Waters ran the mill followed by Stratton who commenced the manufacture of broadcloths. Cochrane indicates the other owners of the mill as being Joseph Hepworth and James Longbotham and later Kirk & Bower. "Robert Spence & Wm McElrath...ran a woolen mill in the building now used by Woolsey Wright as a grist mill, employing fifteen or twenty hands. They came here young men and lived together, in the same house where Figaro Milden now lives, (NB near Dr. Harris's former home and office) until Spence got married. Joseph Hepworth, grandfather of JA Hepworth, also ran the mill for a time".

The 1871 Directory of Ulster County lists "Wright, NW, Marl., Miller"

Cochrane continues, "The village of Marlborough in 1877 is a thriving place, and contains probably fifteen hundred population within a one mile radius of the centre. About seventy-five business concerns exist here and most of them are progressive and enterprising... NW Wright has a flour and grist mill on West Landing street , being assisted in the business by his son, Fred Wright. The mill is a very old one, being the same run by Spence & McElrath as a woolen mill sixty years ago." Landing Street was the name of the road going to the docks from 9W. West Landing Street was the short piece of road from there west of 9W.

In later years Cluett Schantz ran a feed business there.

Nancy and Bill Lyons presently reside near where the original Wright's mill was situated on Old Man's Creek.

How the Kill or creek got its name is grist for a further writing.

A Brief History of Farming in Marlborough

The written history of Marlborough (archeological artifacts predate this) starts with Henry Hudson's trip up, what he named, the "North River" in 1609. In his logs as he passed what is now Marlborough he made note of two outstanding points of land extending into the river - Danskammer on the south and Juffrow's Hook or Blue Point on the north - primarily the northern and southern boundaries of the town of Marlborough.

On his return downstream on Sept. 15 several Native Americans boarded the Half Moon, visited the crew and brought with them some Indian wheat which they sold for "trifles" (remember Manhattan was purchased for roughly $24). This was our first indication of Farming in Marlborough and the first documented agricultural sale.

Legend has it that the Huguenots, before settling New Paltz, stopped at Marlborough. They rejected it as being too rocky to their liking.

In 1695 the crown in England granted to Captain John Evans a tract of land which included Marlborough, Plattekill, Newburgh and New Windsor. Very often as a stipulation in the granting of Patents, the crown would include wording requiring that the land be settled within a period of 5 years. This had a twofold purpose - it brought in extra taxes and it served as a buffer to counteract the strong Dutch population in New York. The English had taken over New York only short time before. In 1699 - over the protests of Evans, the Patent was annulled. The crown declared that Evans had not lived up to the stipulation of settling the tract. Evans declared that, indeed he had settled several families on the tract. One of the settlers Evans claimed was Dennis Relyea, who supposedly had settled near a creek in the area. That creek, ever since, pays homage to old Dennis by being named "Old Man's Creek".

Thus it seems, before the close of the 17th century, Marlboro had its first white settler. Since it is assumed Dennis lived near Old Man's Creek, and since travel by water was the easiest means of transportation in the early years, it may be deduced that Dennis lived somewhere near the hamlet of Marlboro, near the river, though exactly where has never been ascertained.

Did Dennis farm? Probably, for his own food, although certainly not in the grand sense that we farm today.

The first Patent after Evans, in the town of Marlborough, was the Barbarie Patent of 1709 (2000 A in the NE part of town - including the hamlet of Milton) - followed by the Bond Patent in 1710 (600A just below the Barbarie Patent), the Griggs & Graham in 1712 (1200A covered the hamlet of Marlboro), the Morris Patent (3600A, the largest of the patents, in the center of the town including Lattingtown) in 1714 and the Kennedy Patent in 1715 (the SE corner of town as well as on the river between Bond and Griggs and Graham) -

Then there was a stretch of 40 years before the next patent The Harrison Patent in 1750.

Thus it can be seen, the first patents covered the river front from the Paltz Patent or Jeffrow's hook to the S boundary of town, near DansKammer.

Colonel Lewis DuBois who built and lived in the house that bears his name, owned the site of the village of Marlboro. He settled in the town prior to 1760 and owned land on both sides of Old Man's Creek. He was engaged in farming on a large scale and was a noted slave holder.

Edward Hallock, came here from Long Island December 31. 1760 with his wife and children and settled on the Bond Patent

The N part of the Barbarie Patent was bought in 1762 by Leonard Smith. The eldest son Anning built the Smith pond which provided a fall of water 120 feet in height. Here he built a woolen mill, saw mill and grist mill. He also kept a store and from his dock maintained shipping service by sloop.

The S half of the Barbarie Patent was bought by Benjamin Sands in 1776.

Smith and Sands each bought 1000A indicating there was no subdivision of the Patent prior to that time.

You may note, there is indication that farming was in force in Marlborough by the mid 1700s - including grain farming and the raising of sheep which was a big part of the farming in the early years. There was also indication of the river shipping industries and the building of mills and stores. As can be seen, these supported the growth of farming in town as well as were supported by that farming. This was a mutually supportive relationship that has led to the growth of the town of Marlborough.

The leading settlement in the town in the early 1800s was not Marlboro, nor was it Milton - it was Lattingtown. Besides being the center of business activity, it also was the social center and a magnet for those seeking fun and frolic. Horse racing, pugilistic encounters and dances were well attended. There were two hotels and at least one still making apple brandy to help supply their taprooms

An indication of another type of farming in town...- In 1792 the town granted its first liquor licenses for the sum of £2 each. No fewer than nine licenses were taken out In 1793. Folklore indicates that apple brandy or hard apple cider were among the alcoholic beverages of choice.

Isaac Hill, in order to encourage business for his two sloops sailing from the old Powell dock, was an early advocate of the Farmers' Turnpike which built the road extending west from Milton. Quimby and Lewis and Millard & DuBois operated sloops prior to 1830. New York City required great quantities of wood for fuel and sloops from here carried these products. Hay and grain for the city's thousands of horses, butter and livestock were also transported. Milton was at the heart of this shipping and frequently the river would he dotted with fifty or more ships.

Cochrane tells us: "A shopkeeper friend of Edward Young one day in 1834 observed a package on his counter, which he was satisfied had been left by a stranger. He laid the package aside for several days when, it not being called for, he opened it, found some young raspberry plants, and set them out. They yielded such splendid fruit that he sent for his friend Edward Young and invited him to take some and raise them. This was the fall of 1835."

Young took the plants home, propagated them and was very pleased with the results. They proved very prolific, and far ahead in quality of any other variety.

Young was laughed at for trying to sell them in NYC, but time proved his wisdom.

The <u>OC Portrait & Biographical Record</u> has this to say about the Youngs and the Antwerp Raspberry.

"Edward Young...was born about 1780 in the town of Marlboro. ... His main occupation was farming, and he was the first man in the township to engage in fruit-raising and the first to sell apple-trees in Marlboro. He was also the one who introduced the Antwerp raspberry to the attention of fruit-growers in that vicinity. ..."

PICKING RASPBERRIES
(from Harpers Weekly Jul. 26, 1873 p 646)

Edward was one of the largest of the early fruit growers in the town and introduced the famous Antwerp raspberry to the New York market around 1838. The fruit became so popular there that cultivation "put Marlborough on the map as a fruit growing section" and brought a great deal of wealth to the industry.

The Antwerp raspberry was first introduced into the town of Marlborough, Ulster County, New York, in 1835 by Mr. Thomas Burling, who obtained it at New Rochelle. The culture of this delicious fruit soon acquired importance. Before many years every farmer in the township had his raspberry patch, and the culture was attempted in adjacent towns. These attempts were only partially successful, except in Cornwall, Newburgh, and Highland, which, with Marlborough, occupy a stretch of territory seventeen miles in length on the west bank of the Hudson. The soil about these towns seems to be peculiarly adapted to the culture of the raspberry. Strawberries, blackberries, and currants are also raised there in great quantities.

Raspberry picking begins the latter part of June and closes early in August. The pickers, as shown in our illustration on page 644, are chiefly young men and women, who hail the season with delight, as the work is regarded as a sort of prolonged spree. The getting together of so many young people makes the fields cheerful and inviting, and evenings, when work is done, merry with song and dance.

In the fields each person has a "picker" - a kind of box with short legs and a hoop handle, capable of holding sixteen cups. As these pickers are filled they are taken to the packing house, where the "packers" look them over, and place the cups in large boxes, or sometimes crates, holding all the way from thirty to ninety cups. As each box or crate is filled, it is locked and directed to whatever commission merchant in New York may have engaged them, and every afternoon from five to eight o'clock the berries picked through the day are taken to the docks, thence to the city by steamer. The berries we have today should have been growing on the bushes yesterday.

Years vary considerably as regards the amount of berries raised, owing partly to the season, but mostly to the quantity of dressing used to strengthen the soil. In 1865, from June 23 to August 8, there were shipped from Marlboro dock 1,216,765 cups, and almost the same number from Milton dock, which is in Marlborough. In 1866, from June 20 to August 10, 807,158 cups were sent away. Now in 1867 the yield surpassed that of 1865, there having been shipped form June 24 to August 11, 1,295,693 cups. In 1868, there was a falling off to 869,388 cups, from June 25 to August 9; then in 1869 to 517,975. This decrease woke the "growers" up, and the good attention they gave to their fields was rewarded by a yield of nearly 1,000,000 of cups, and in 1871 more than 1,500,000 cups were sent away. This year the crop is very poor, owing partly to the lack of rain and partly to bad cultivation."

Michael Wygant, grandson of the original colonist, (who came to Newburgh in 1709) was the first Wygant to come to Marlborough. His left his three sons; James, Michael and John adjoining farms in West Marlborough. James's son Clemence and grandsons Foster and J. Calvin became prominent fruit growers and were also responsible for the growth of the industry. The Hepworth name first appears in business annals of the town during the early 1800s. J. A. Hepworth, was primarily interested in farming and fruit growing. J Augustus settled down to become one of our leading fruit growers, cultivating the Antwerp raspberries and introducing new varieties of fruit.

Historically, not all farmers had large farms. And not all farmers had hired help. From a letter from Wm. Nicklin to his father in May of 1872.

"My strawberries are most plentiful and show the best of any. I hope to do good by them. I have grafted me more choice apples and put in more grapes with hundreds of cherry currants. I raise all my plants etc., do all my own grafting, training, etc. Sowed last week 3 acres oats and sowed some fields to clover. This I hired out. I do wish you could be here in Berry Time. All is hustle and work, no times to play then. It would surprise you to see the lines of Berry Wagons - they load two large steamboats every night in season. Here my children count. It will take my wife, 4 children and two smart pickers besides, to pick mine this season and I put out a new patch next week.

The old Hallock mill, with its beginnings in the early 1800s ground grain for nearly a century....Foster Hallock founded the mill in 1808 or 1809 and for many years it specialized in grinding buckwheat, of which large quantities were produced by local farmers. For several years before the mill was given up in 1936 it had been used by R. W. Hallock and son as a cider mill and vinegar plant.

In the mid 1800s Irish immigrants began coming to Marlborough in large numbers. At first most of them worked on farms or in industry but soon they began buying land for themselves. The proportion of people of Irish extraction operating farms became very large after 1875. Shortly thereafter came the Germans, encouraged to come here to work in the fruit. Some 2000 or more came every year and stayed through the harvest. They were hard working, but enjoyed patronizing the saloons after their day's work. They made a road down past the McMullen buildings (now the Raccoon Saloon) north of the Farmer's hotel where they established an attractive beer garden on the hill overlooking the ravine and the river. For many years farmers depended upon these immigrants to help harvest their crops.

Italian immigration came beginning in the 1890's. Word of mouth of this productive fruit growing area drew thousands experienced in fruit growing and harvesting. Many of them had just arrived from Italy and looked upon this as the "promised land" in the "promised land". The old Marlborough winery attracted hundreds of Italian immigrants to come to work in Marlborough. Many bought land as soon as they could. Many brought with them the skills necessary to make robust wines and the home brewing of wines became an ancillary activity.

Perhaps the greatest fruit marketing organization in the eastern part of the state, the Hudson River Fruit Exchange, was organized in 1912 with Wm. Velie the leading promoter. A gross business of $40,000 was done the first year. The steady growth is reflected by the total sales of $505,000 in 1930. Besides helping to market fresh fruits and distributing supplies to local farmers, the Exchange operated cherry pitting and currant freezing plants, and had an interest in the Milton cold storage. In 1936 the organization sold the entire grape crops from 189 farms in bulk packages to fill orders for jelly and juice and wineries. It also sold and processed 300 tons of grapes, removed stems. seeds and skins, packed the cooked pulp in 50 gallon barrels and froze it for buyers. Grower-members received $50 a ton net for their grapes from $5 to $10 more than the prevailing price at the time.

During World War I, many farmers had difficulty finding help to harvest their crops. The government encouraged getting them help by initiating the "Farmerettes" program. These were young women answering their country's call and filling in on the home front. Several of the local farmers married several of these "Farmerettes" and they have thus contributed to our local gene pool.

In the mid 1900s, as automobiles proved more reliable and roads greatly improved, the entire area was opened up to tourists who often would spend their summer vacations at local boarding houses. At one time, there were a good number of these establishments in town. The increase in automobile traffic and the number of people either staying in or passing through town gave rise to the roadside fruit stand. Local roads, especially 9W, became dotted with these stands which proved to be a lucrative outlet for the farmers' produce.

Ed McGowan bought the property of the Marlborough Fruit Growers, Inc. and years he had contracts for supplying Bartlett pears and other fruits for making baby foods at the Beechnut plant. He processed and sold small fruit for preserve making plants in Philadelphia, New York and Jersey and supplied great quantities of apples and other fruit to chain stores.

Migrant workers in orchard (circa 1970)

In later years, farmers employed a large number of migrants to help harvest their crops. Many were cotton workers from the South. They began to come to town every harvest season and many farmers put up small structures to house them during the season. Often these clustered structures were known as "migrant camps". Their need for religious services was recognized. Miss Lula Clarke and her brother Walter Clarke of Milton were active in the 1940's organizing a summer church for migrants. Services were at first held in the Marlborough Presbyterian church, then in the old Friends Meeting House at Milton, and later in the little wooden Gothic building at Milton which was All Saints Episcopal Church.

The G.L.F. market in Milton. was organized as a cooperative. It ran an auction which attracted hundreds of buyers to its property just north of Milton. The buildings were erected and local business started in 1941. The auction business was a big feature for years and during 1942 and 1943 sales of $700,000 to $800,000 were reported,

Joe DallVechia entered the trucking business in Marlboro as a young man in an old truck. After awhile, he was utilizing a fleet of trucks to bring fruit to New York City. He produced vast quantities of cider and vinegar and transported these products to the New York area in huge tank trucks. His contribution to the area was the market afforded fruit growers for their inferior grade apples.

Red's Empty Package of Milton was another indicator of the importance of the fruit industry to the Marlborough area. Operated by Red Prezziosi, it started with sales of about 250,000 packages with one truck in 1947 to about from four to five million packages with eight trucks doing deliveries. His business as distributor and supplier of many types of packages was recognized as the largest in Eastern New York

You will note that as well as writing of farming, I have also indicated trends in shipping, basketing, marketing and other facets of enterprise that coexist with farming. Marlborough has never existed on farming alone. However, what I hope has been obvious is that the symbiotic relationship between farming and packaging, cold storage, co-ops, shipping and sales is what has led to Marlborough's economic well being. Today with the growth of pick-your-own farms, tree farms, and nurseries comes the need to meet the demands of agri-tourism. This includes ensuring we have fine and numerous restaurants, Bed and Breakfasts, parks, eclectic shops and activities to support those who would visit Marlborough to taste of our fruits.

Report compiled from Cochrane, Woolsey, Plank and Mahan Histories of Marlborough, the Orange County Portrait and Biographical Record, Harpers Weekly, town historical and personal files

You Light up my Life...

If you lived in Marlborough at the turn of the century - the 19th to the 20th century, that is - undoubtedly you would immediately associate those words with one man, George A Badner.

(Cartoon sketch of 1898 George Badner)
Courtesy of George Badner, Newburgh, NY

It was in 1898 that George A Badner provided the first electricity to the hamlet of Marlboro. "William McKinley was in the White House and a dollar fifty a day was considered excellent wages." At first it was three street lights, reports his grandson, George Badner of Newburgh. The street lights had to be manually turned on at dusk and manually turned off at the end of the service period.

"The Marlborough Electric Company initiated the electric service.

Mr. Badner and only one helper were the operating, commercial, engineering, construction, purchasing and accounting departments. Alone they constructed, maintained and serviced their system", according to a 1957 Central Hudson pamphlet. "They built a small dam on the kill and installed a generator to make use of the existing water power".

Marlborough's first electric station

This, Marlborough's first substation, served the customers of the Marlborough Electric Company. Conduits housed power lines coming from the generator at a nearby stream. The substation was 2 story brick about 15 square feet. It was on the north side of Birdsall Ave., west of the Middle School according to Joe McCourt in a recent telephone interview

The present George Badner said they had a kerosene generator to create electricity when the water flow didn't provide enough power. At first only people in the center of Marlboro had service, a few stores and the three street lights. Service was limited to certain hours of the day and early evening.

Mr. Badner and his helper put up the poles, strung the lines and connected the services. During the early days the wires were strung only 15 or 20 feet high and thus two men could handle the necessary, relatively short poles. Wires were very often attached to the sides of buildings and poles were used primarily to run wires across roadways. Several older houses in Marlboro, in their walls or in their attics, still have the early electric insulators used.

Carl Badner, son of George (who set up the first electricity in Marlboro) reported that his father obtained all his knowledge of electricity by reading books and "tinkering around". He had a keen sense of what electric power would hold for the future.

ELECTRIC LIGHT

PRICES.

The prices to be charged for electric lighting are a combination of contract and meter rates. Each customer will pay a capacity charge of twenty cents per lamp per month, and in addition will pay for current consumed at the extremely low rate of ten cents per Kilowatt hour by meter.

A discount of one cent per Kilowatt hour will be allowed if bill is paid within ten days after presentation. A Kilowatt hour will supply a sixteen candle lamp for eighteen to twenty hours.

Applications received by

GEO. A. BADNER,

Marlborough, N. Y.

(Badner AD)
From Oct. 31, 1902 edition of the Marlborough Record.
Note in this ad the price of electricity was in part determined by the number of lights one had.

There was no interconnections with any other electric companies. George Badner sold the business in 1901 to the Newburgh Light, Heat and Power Company, but took employment with that company and was responsible for the area from Roseton to Milton. The Newburgh Light, Heat and Power Company was the first unit of Central Hudson Gas and Electric Corporation.

The first substation was replaced in 1911 with (according to Joe McCourt) the brick building on Western Avenue, now a residence.

2nd Marlborough substation

In a 1970 Central Hudson pamphlet, there is a report on the "new transformer" being brought into Marlboro.

(photo of "new transformer" being brought thru Marlboro)
"Back in 1911, the gentleman in the derby and his work crew stopped their horse-drawn trailer to oblige a photographer"

This 1911 picture depicts a newer, larger transformer being hauled to the "new" substation. This "new" substation was built for about $5,000. Badner's original generator was later moved to Montgomery Street in Newburgh, one of the earliest electric generating stations in the country. Badner remained an employee of Central Hudson until his death in 1922. Badner's son, Carl, also worked for Central Hudson as did his grandson, George, who retired from Central Hudson a few years ago.

Chillura Boarding House

To: Joseph Canestro <canestro@bnl.gov>
From: MaryLou Mahan, Town of Marlborough, NY
<maryloumahan2004@yahoo.com>
cc: Cindy Lanzetta <cinpackback@yahoo.com>

Hi,

You recently contacted Cindy Lanzetta re the Chillura Bros. Boarding House in Marlborough, NY. I am the Town of Marlborough Historian, and hope I can give you a bit of information you may be searching. Seems to me, your questions boil down to:

1) Where it is (or was) located;
2) Some history of the place; and
3) The approximate date when it closed and ceased doing business.

1)   Attached find a jpg of our town tax map. On it I have indicated in red, exactly where the property is located. The green road (on the map) to which it is adjacent is Lattingtown Road. I trust from there you can find it on almost any map of the community.

2)   As far as history. I can trace it back to the original patent in 1714, but suspect that's not the history that is of interest to you. The property from about 1823 to 1894 was 137 acres, until 37 acres was sold off in 1894. In 1894 Cornelius D Bloomer was the owner and he sold the property to William H Free of Newburgh. The price at that time was $8,000 - it is listed as being "a farm". In 1897 Free sold

the land back to Cornelius Bloomer. At this time the selling price was listed as $1 - just enough to make it legal.

In 1909 Cornelius D Bloomer and his wife sold the land to Charles Blaison of Marlborough. Since I am going by deeds, and many times deeds do not specify if there are buildings or not, it is almost impossible to say what buildings may have been on the property at this time. It is suspected that at least an old barn were part of the property deeded.

In a 1959 pamphlet on the History of Marlborough, Will Plank, who was owner of our local newspaper and quite an impressive historian wrote:

"The tide of Italian immigration began in the 1890's but did nor reach its peak until the twenties when reports of this prolific fruit growing region drew thousands of industrious people experienced in fruit culture. Many of them had just arrived from Italy and looked upon this as the promised land. They bought farms and made rocky, brush-covered hillsides the old settlers had considered waste land blossom like a rose. Unquestionably these hard-working citizens have done more to increase the productivity of much of our land than one would have considered possible. When growing fruit and vegetables and cultivating the vine these people have few equals and many have become equally good business men."

The Marano brothers were among the first Italians to locate here about 1890. Others came in slowly until some twenty years later Perrino of the old Marlborough winery induced hundreds to come work in the fruit. Many bought land as soon as they could, but the great bulk of the immigrant, naturalized or second generation Italians came here to buy property and develop it. During the twenties when this region enjoyed its greatest real estate boom about 90% of the land sold was to these new citizens and now they are among the leaders in many lines of endeavor.

We see the above property sold in 1912 (for $12,500 as a farm) to Antonia Leto, Gristina Chillura, Giuseppina Massaro and John Leto with the following added: "The above premises are conveyed to parties of the second part in the proportion that the said Antonia Leto & Gristina Chillura are each the owners of the undivided 2/6 part thereof and the said Giusoppina Massaro & John Leto are each the owners of the undivided 1/6 part thereof"

In 1914 Gristina is deeded the total property and in 1922 the property is deeded to Antonio and Demenico Chillura - totalling about 100 acres.

I believe it is about this period that Chillura Bros. began to build - both with respect to buildings and with respect to clientelle. For many years they enjoyed a reputation as a fine boarding house. As pictures show, there was a swimming pool, a lake for boating and tennis courts as well as other amenities. See the attached which is a copy of a post card showing the Chillura tennis court.

3) In 1967 the property was sold to Joseph Garcia. I believe Garcia still ran the business for a few years. In an e/mail that I got in 2004 from Richard Hayes (his e/mail address at that time <rhayes1@optonline.net>) he writes:

"I used to go there as a kid. I worked there one summer as a waiter and busboy. Joe Garcia was the owner of the property, he was like an uncle to me.

I spoke with George Wygant who lived on the property in the early 1990s. He indicated at that time most of the buildings were still standing. The swimming pool was there, though in disrepair. In the early 1990's, there was an auction held of the remaining excess furniture, etc.

From an interview that Paul Faurie did with Ollie Mackey (a Chillura Bros. neighbor) Aug. 26, 1988.

Paul - Right next door was the Chillura place. Did they always own that?
Ollie - They got it in 1900 - round that time.
Paul - That was the family boarding house at one time.
Ollie - A minister (?) lived there before that. I don't know his name.
Paul - Was that part of this farm?
Ollie - No, that was separate - a quarter
Paul - Ran a big boarding house for many years.
Ollie - On a weekend during the war they had 1000 people when they couldn't get any gas.

Jean - Sale on Sept. 10, always a family
Paul - Christine LoBurgio is executive of the place (Christine was a Chillura daughter).
(NB Christine LoBurgio taught school at the Marlboro Elementary School for many years. Chris died in Dec. 1997 - MLM)

Ben Chillura (a son) had a home on Plattekill Road right near the present Marlborough High School. For many years he was a realtor in Marlboro. My husband was friendly with Ben Chillura's son-in-law, Chuck Whipper.

My son has been at the property (c 1990) and was impressed with the tree lined approach and the natural surround. Apparently the old barn was being redone and turned into a dwelling house - the results are quite noteworthy. The barn is reputedly quite old (i.e. early 1800s).

Don't know how much of this you wanted, or if this is what you wanted. Let me know whether or not this satisfies you and we can take it from there.

Respectfully,
MaryLou Mahan
Town of Marlborough Historian

VILLA CHILLURA Bros.
Marlboro, N. Y.
Phone 29 F. 12 - Summer Service 104

Remembrances of a Summer Boarder

As town historian, one often gets phone calls of inquiry. Often it's someone searching for their forebears "...born in 1766, do you know his parents?" This phone call was from Florida and very interesting as it was from a woman who had spent some five or six summers in Marlborough when she was a young girl. Her memories were so favorable that she was desirous of visiting again. Unfortunately, it was over 50 years ago and thus she didn't know where to find the place on a present day map.

The woman was Emily Wiseman ne Motta. Her parents were John and Mary. Her father was a chef in New York City and sent his wife and daughter to Marlborough in order for them to experience "rural life" during the hot summers. He commuted to Marlborough every weekend to be with his family.

Emily vividly remembered walking up the road about 1/4 mile to go swimming in a neighborhood pool where there was also a refreshment stand. They would walk about 1/2 mile in the opposite direction to obtain milk from a farmer who kept cows. My mind was whirling, but I couldn't think where this might be. Imagine my surprise when she said the owner of the summer boarding house was Peter Vari. Pete had lived just down the road from me - he is since deceased. She was pleased that she was able to find where she had spent her summers and set an appointment for a visit - a visit she said she had been desirous of making for several years.

When contacted, the present residents of the Vari homestead, the Mauros, agreed to let us visit the homestead. As might be expected, Emily had remembered the place as being much bigger and the distances between the pool and the cows much more extensive. She was, after all a young girl at that time, and we all know the tricks that our minds play on us when we "remember when...."

She seemed genuinely pleased to see the place again and pointed out the sign that was still there, the stable where Pete Vari kept his horse (the horse named, "Charlie" always had his head out the window), and, what had been the dining room and kitchen. She pointed to a spot on the lawn and said it was in that corner that she learned to rake.

Emily Wiseman and Vari Farm sign

We then went down the road (by no means 1/2 mile!) and visited with Mel and Gloria Alonge. Gloria invited us into her cozy dining room and we sat around the table waiting for Mel to arrive. Emily told the story of walking the road one day with her friend and seeing a particularly luscious looking pear decided to pick it though it was rather high in the tree. Imagine their surprise when a hand came from the interior of the tree and said, "Here take this one, it's easier". She said they were so scared they ran home. She remembers the young man, who was on a ladder picking fruit from the tree as having dark, curly hair and being very good looking.

Enter Mel Alonge and she immediately recognized him as being that young man - though his hair is no longer dark.

There was a good discussion around that dining room table.

Talk about Pete Vari having been a chef at St. George's Hotel in Manhattan and coming to Marlborough with his wife, Ida.

The pool was at Treccariche's - (presently DiMonsi) and, yes, there was a refreshment stand as well as a dance hall. Mel said many Saturday nights were spent at the dance hall where there was often live music - Mel especially remembering the accordion player. Emily said she learned to swim in that pool.

Emily remembered going to St. Mary's every week for services.

The Varis charged $35 per week - and that included three meals a day. Mel winked and added, "Wine was extra". Pete Vari had a reputation of being an excellent wine maker.

Emily also remembered helping to pick currants and tomatoes on Vari's farm. She said, in later years, twice she had won canning sweepstakes - she credited her experience with tomatoes in Marlborough as being the inspiration.

Emily chuckled as she recalled taking the wash down a farm road on Alonge's farm to a small spring where they washed their clothes. She mentioned having to lug the washboard to and from the spring.

Mel's mother had goats and cows and sold the milk as well as cheese she had made.

Mel said it was a wonderful time to remember. It was a small community and there was a lot of visiting back and forth - especially among the Italian families who lived in the area.

As we left Mel's home we noted a fig tree he carefully tends in his front yard. Gloria says he enjoys fruit from the tree for many months during the summer. In the winter he carefully packs it into his garage to yield again the following year.

Mel, Emily and fig tree

As we took leave, Emily again expressed her pleasure at being able to "return to yesteryear" and told us these were some of the best days of her life and she remembered with great affection her time in Marlborough and the many wonderful people she met and experiences she had.

Makes one wonder - how many other people in far flung places in this world still carry a piece of Marlborough with them and smile to themselves and feel a warming in their hearts as they remember their time in that quaint little town up the Hudson?

Update from a previous story - got a call from Adele Lyons - she remembers reading the story, "The Lost Gold Mine of the Hudson", to her students when she taught school several years ago. Adele said she thinks she had to borrow the book from the New York State Library at that time. Adele is well remembered for exposing her students to good literature and sparking an interest in reading. That's another pebble dropped in the pond whose ripples keep on growing and going.

Forget the Chads

I suspect we're all glad that the election is finally over. We all breathed a sigh of relief that there was not the contention over the actual results that plagued us in 2000. Thought the readers might be interested in some of the historical perspectives on elections.

The original town records on elections are rather sparse.

At a precinct meeting held at the house of Nehemiah Denton in and for the precinct of Newburgh the first Tuesday in April in the year of our Lord one thousand seven hundred and sixty eight according to an act of Assembly:

> Leonard Smith chosen Clerk
>
> Edward Hallock - Supervisor
>
> Arthur Smith, Latting Carpenter, Marcus Ostranders Assessors

At a town meeting held at Henry Deyo's on April ye 7, 1772 for the Precinct of New Marlborough according to the Act of Assembly for the Province of New York in meeting Assembled:

> Clerk - Abijah Perkins

Supervisor - Lewis DuBois

Assessors - Jacob Wood, Marcus Ostrander

At the annual Town meeting for the Precinct of New Marlborough held on April the 6, 1773 was chosen by plurality of votes:

Clerk - Abijah Perkins

Supervisor - Lewis DuBois

Assessors - Joseph Mory, Jeremiah Mackey

After the American Revolution we find the following wordings:

From the following it might be assumed the votes were cast by ayes and nays, (or is it proper to say, "He voiced his concerns via letter"?)

At a precinct meeting held at Capt. Silas Purdy's on April ye 7th 1778 for the precinct of New Marlborough according to an Act of Assembly there was then and there chosen by a majority of voices the following town officers for this precinct year, viz.:

Clerk - Stephen Case

Supervisor - Elijah Lewis

The following was the oath sworn to by John Davis, elected Constable:

I, John Davis, do solemnly swear and declare in the presence of Almighty God that I will bear true faith and allegiance to the State of New York as a free and independent State and that I will in all things to the best of my knowledge and ability do my duty as a good subject of the said state ought to do - signed before Wolvert Ecker, Justice

July ye 12th 1779 This is to certify the following persons have taken the oath of Allegiance to the States of America as is prescribed - Caleb Merritt, Jacob Wood, Jeremiah Howell, Silas Purdy & William Thorne - sworn before Benjamin Carpenter, Justice of the Peace

At a town meeting held at Latting Town on April ye 4th, 1780 for the precinct of New Marlborough according to Act of Assembly there was then and there chosen by a majority of voices the following town officers and regulations for this present year, also at an adjoined meeting held ye 18th of April 1780 when the whole officers were chosen to serve for this year:

Stephen Case - Clerk and poor master

Anning Smith - Supervisor

It was in 1799 that the first votes were recorded for Senate:

A list of candidates voted for Senators for the middle district taken at election in the town of Marlborough 1799:

The number of votes for James Oliver - ninety-eight

The number of votes for Samuel Augustus Barker - thirty six

The number of votes for Isaac Bloom - forty seven

The number of votes for John Suffren - seventeen

The number of votes for John Hathorn - seventy five

The number of votes for Jesse Thompson - thirty six

The number of votes for Moses Thompson - two

We do hereby certify the above to be a true estimate of votes taken for the above named persons May 3, 1799 - Cornelius Drake, Peter McCoun, David Staples, William Drake and Thaddeus Hait - Inspectors of Election

This is rather impressive when one realizes that according to the 1800 assessment list, there were 220 landholders in the town. It's not known for how many candidates a voter could vote.

The first record for votes for governor was in 1801:

Statement of votes taken at the Anniversary Election for Governor, Lieutenant Governor and Senators which commenced on the last Tuesday of April one thousand eight hundred and one:

George Clinton - Governor - 62 votes

Stephen Van Renselear - 32 votes

James Watson - Lieutenant Governor - 32 votes

Jeremiah Van Renselear - Lieutenant Governor - 62 votes

Statement of votes taken in the town of Marlborough for delegates to the Convention to be held in the City of Albany the second Tuesday of October next; the election commenced on the last Tuesday of August 1801:

John Cantine - 66 votes

Anning Smith - 73 votes

Abraham Schoonmaker - 68 votes

Lucas Elmendorf - 66 votes

Jonathan Hasbrook - 10 votes

Moses Cantine Jur - 5 votes

George Wartz - 3 votes

Interestingly in 1804 in a vote for Governor, Morgan Lewis received 84 votes and Aaron Burr received 32 votes from the freeholders in

Marlborough. Burr didn't fare too well in Marlborough, possibly because he was involved in the court case between Patentees in Marlborough and the Duzine in New Paltz that eventually settled the boundary between Marlborough and what is now the Town of Lloyd.

Burr was elected a senator from New York State in 1791. He served six years and later won a seat in the state legislature when he was not re-elected to the Senate. After the loss of his seat in the legislature in 1799, he began to organize the Democratic Party in New York City. The group became a political power that hoped to ensure the election of a democratic President. The ticket was to be Thomas Jefferson as President and Aaron Burr as Vice-President. The wrangling of the "politicos" ended in a draw — both men received seventy-three electoral votes each. Jefferson and Burr were not really fond of one another and in New York — Alexander Hamilton decided to use his weight and influence to support Thomas Jefferson — who was elected. After unsuccessfully attempting to gain the presidency, Burr eventually was nominated in 1804 to the governorship of New York, but lost to Republican Morgan Lewis. Each loss he blamed on Alexander Hamilton. On July 11, 1804 — Burr and Hamilton met at ten paces, both fired and Hamilton fell, mortally wounded.

William W. Mackey

On another note: During an interview with Stella Mackey several years ago she noted about her grandfather William W. Mackey that he had had very strong political views. He took to the trail and campaigned for Grover Cleveland in Pennsylvania and New York.

Beers in his <u>Biographical Record of Ulster County</u> (1896) notes:

"Mr. Mackey is an ardent advocate of Republican principles, having supported the party since its organization, and in 1856 made many political speeches in Pennsylvania".

Stella continued by saying during Cleveland's second campaign, William W. vowed not to shave until Cleveland won the election.

Cleveland lost and William W. wore a long flowing beard that reached to his midsection to the day he died. Stella remembers seeing him in his coffin with his long white beard. Apparently, for his political prowess and efforts William W was made Post Master of Lattingtown. Yes, there was a Post Office in Lattingtown! Stella remembers playing with the letter files as a child.

Until after the Civil War only adult free males were permitted to vote. Who the first Black in Marlborough to cast a vote was has not been discovered in the records. If anyone has any information relative to this, I would love to hear of it.

Voting in those bygone days was not a trivial task. One couldn't stop by on the way home from work, or jump in the car and take the five minute ride to town. One had to catch the horse (if one was lucky enough to own a horse), saddle it and ride it to the voting place.

On Nov. 7, 1872 Susan B Anthony was fined for attempting to vote in an election. It is believed she never paid the fine. She did, however, acknowledge the support the Women's Suffrage Movement had received from one of Marlborough's own.

Written on "National Woman Suffrage Association" stationery:

Rochester, NY
June 25, 1887

My Dear Miss Hull,

On this lovely June morning in a pile of old envelopes - addressed and stamped, I came to this ??? to your dear sister and my most excellent friend, Sarah H Hallock. The date of the envelope shows that the thought of her was several years ago!

It seems impossible to see your lovely home among the vines there without dear Sarah in it, though it is many years since I saw her there. My last glimpse of her was in the press of a Washington Convention 3 or 4 years ago.

When I first heard of her passage to the beyond I fully intended to write you of my love and admiration of the one gone and my sympathy for the lonely one left in that beautiful hillside home, but alas the days are not long enough for me to do the half of the needful things I am prompted to do - so to very many of my best friends I seem to be forgetful if not ungrateful. But I shall not forget your bright, beautiful, clear-sighted sister, Sarah, nor your own dear self, while memory lasts. I wish she could have remained over to be with us in the celebration of the fortieth anniversary of the first Woman's Right's Convention.

She was at the third one at Worcester two years later, while I was at home on my dear father's Rochester farm reading the report of it in the New York Daily Tribune.

Very few of those who stood for the grand principle two score of years ago are now left. I hope you will be able to attend the Council.

With Love & Sympathy
Yours as ever,

Susan B. Anthony

The Milton library has been named for the above Sarah Hull Hallock. While Sarah never had the opportunity to vote, one of the first, if not the first woman to vote in Marlborough was Ernestine Wygant.

She had arrived in Marlborough just a short time before Election Day in order to take up her new position as teacher at the Marlborough High School. She was just 22 years old.

Her first job was teaching English, French and music. She traveled here by train on September 6, 1920,

Ernestine Wygant

having to change trains in Boston and arriving in Marlboro in the dark of evening. She remembers the sensation of winding up and up and up in the taxi, wondering when she would reach the top. She stayed with the principal, Mr. Taylor and his wife at their home (later the Plank's house).

This year, Americans turned out in larger than expected numbers to cast their ballots. This is a tribute, not only to those who "got out the vote", not only the candidates who campaigned so vigorously, but also to our forebears to whom the vote was a very "special" privilege of being an American.

Thars Gold in them Thar Hills

It is impossible to tell where the rumors got started, but they have led to many an interesting legend to be told and retold.

While some early patents retained the rights to various "treasures" such as trees of a certain girth and mineral rights, many of the early patents within the township of Marlborough granted "all and singular woods, underwoods, trees, ..., meadow marshes, ... streams of water, fishing, fowling, hawking, hunting, mines and minerals, standing, growing, lying and being to be used, had and enjoyed within ye limits..." (Bond Patent of 1710 from Queen Ann)

There were snatches of lore of the pirate, Captain Kidd, stashing some treasures in the Hudson Valley and it was during these early days in the history of Marlborough that the legend began to emerge of gold mines that had been worked by the Native Americans, their whereabouts, naturally, were always a secret. The lure of gold and treasure, nonetheless, enticed many an adventurer to seek his fortune in a lost or buried treasure.

Tristram Coffin, in 1915, took many remnants of these stories and wove them into a delightful tale of adventure and daring. The story is set in the Hudson Valley. Tristram writes of the mountains,

Tristram Coffin House - Sands Ave. Milton

141

"The one (range) nearest the river and only a few miles from it comprises a number of thickly wooded hills, varying in height from 700 to 1000 feet above the sea level...For many miles they stand like sentinels guarding the long-settled region that lies between them and the Hudson". His description of the small hamlet of "Knotlimb" is a thinly veiled reference to Milton. His story starts with an old recluse with a Native American friend. Together they make stealthy trips into the mountains. It is not until the recluse dies that it is discovered he has a treasure of gold hidden in his humble abode. The story then continues with the adventures of two young lads who determine to find the source of the treasure. You can read this exciting story at either of Marlborough's libraries, or the book is available for purchase in neighboring bookstores.

Gold in them thar hills? You shake your head and think, "Most unlikely". However, there have been a number of our forebears who gave credence to the possibility.

Early on there must have been some treasure hunting in the southern end of Marlborough as in a deed of 1820 John Canfield writes into the deed, "Party of the first shall have the liberty to dig in the hole or mine so called a little southwest of the dwelling house at any time or to employ who he pleases to dig in said mine during the term of ten years and, if anything is found valuable in the said mine, then the said mine to belong to the said party of the first part and to his heirs forever."

In the western part of town in 1825 Michael Wygant sold 1 3/4 acres to Robert Harris, "mines and minerals excepted."

A similar deed in 1833 in the northern end of town declares, "Excepting and reserving all mines and minerals." This was in a deed from David Mackey to the Conklins. Moreover, the rights excepted persisted through the next deed where it is explicitly written, "Reserving out of the above lands all mines and minerals which may hereafter be discovered on or in said lands unto David Mackey, his heirs and assigns forever - subject nevertheless to all damages incurred in working said mines to be paid to the said George Harper."

The Mackeys did try their hand at mining. In the 1959 "Fifty Niner" John Matthews has a picture of the "Mackey mine hole"

Again in 1833 and again in the southern end of town Joseph Lockwood sold the mineral rights to his property.

In consideration of covenants and agreements hereinafter contained - the coals, ores, fossils, minerals and rocks containing mineral substances of whatever name or nature situate, laying and being under, in or upon my lands Together with the right of digging, boring, blasting, mining, excavating, raising and carrying off said coals, ores, fossils, minerals and substances

The legend started many years ago, some say prior to the American Revolution. We've seen documentation that there were hopes for profitable mines in the early 1800's. The Mackeys did their mining in the late 1800's. Tristram Coffin wrote his story in 1915. Warren Sherwood, a local historian also treated stories of the lost gold mine. John Matthews wrote in the 1950's.

Thus it's seen that the legend persists. To my knowledge, no gold has been found in Marlborough, but, hey, you never know!

Of Other Times
Round the Pot Belly

Sam Quimby, Jack Baldwin, Mike Canosa

It was a miserable day! It was raining and the temperature was hovering just above freezing - not the kind of day one expects to be able to lure Senior Citizens from the warmth and comforts of their homes. Thanks to the Milton Library the coffee was on. Cookies were obtained from the new Milton Bakery. We'd set up a paper representation of a Pot Belly stove complete with candle to furnish the suggestive warmth of the fire. And they came - Sam Quimby, Jack Baldwin, Mike Canosa, Adele Woolsey Lyons, Howard Quimby, Carol Wygant Felter, Stanley Baxter and Jim Kent. Joe and Jeannie McCourt arrived later. It was unusual for me to be one of the "youngsters" of the group.

We gathered to share our memories of Marlboro and Milton and one had to be impressed with how vivid the memories were. As each story was shared, it was most apparent that these folks, who mostly had spent their entire lives in the community, were committed to

Marlborough, its people and its history. It's not possible to cover all that transpired so here is a sampling.

How a flat tire changed the course of one family's destiny - Jack Baldwin reported that he and his family were returning from a trip north to visit "the country". As tires were wont to do in those days, one of the tires went flat right near a sand bank. As his father was changing the tire, his mother, grandmother and grandfather alighted from the car. They spied a sign nearby that said "For Sale". His father inquired and shortly thereafter his family were the proud possessors of an 80 acre farm - 40 acres on each side of the road.

Jack reported that the house had no running water, no electricity and no central heating. It had been owned by three spinsters named Barnes. His father had had no experience in farming. The father bought 2 horses, hired 2 men and began to clear the fields. He and the men planted apple and peach trees. Jack mused that he thought his father had the idea that after the trees started bearing fruit he would become a "gentleman farmer".

For a while they rented the farm to Abe Smith - a house and 80 acres of farm land for $125 per month. His father had had to borrow $300 from the Marlboro bank that was managed by Ed Carpenter at that time.

When they decided to make the move permanent, Jack remembers coming up one foggy night in a truck over Storm King Mountain with buffalo robes over them. It was February. Jack entered school. In April, his father took sick with the grip. The father's conditioned worsened and he died a few days later. The trees hadn't been pruned. Twenty or thirty of the neighbors got together and helped the family prune the trees and dispose of the brush. Jack said it took all spring. One of Velie's men came up to help. They also planted 500 tomato plants and sold tomatoes and peaches that year - for $.45 for 1/2 bushel of peaches. They were able to put apples in Velie's cooler and later in the season were able to realize $.75 per box. Many years later Jack still remembers the kindness shown by the neighbors who pitched in and helped.

The lawyer helping the family through the legal requisites in settling the estate was Henry Kohl. Henry Kohl lost his wife and after some time Henry Kohl married Jack's widowed mother.

Jack remembers how difficult farming was - long hours, all kinds of weather, the fruit not bringing much money - and, on occasion, the weather tossed a monkey wrench as the year the hail stones were so bad they dented and all but ruined the apple crop.

Soon the Baldwins were sending the apples to Boston and the price of apples went up to $1.75 or $2.00. They were able to buy a truck and a car. They bought a Ford tractor from Sunstrom's garage in Marlboro for $800 - which was a lot of money for them.

Later Baldwins were able to clear a field and build the fruit stand that has become a landmark on 9W. Jack noted life was not always easy for the family, but, because of the neighbors and friends and family, he would, given the choice, do the same things all over again. He said, "It was a good life."

We discussed various "interesting people" who had lived in town. Carol Felter told a story her father told her that when Greaves, who lived next to the bakery, was offered a cigar he said, "No thanks, but I'll take a newspaper." The Van Buskirk twins were brought up - they enjoyed imbibing and holding heated discussions while sitting on their front porch - the whole town would hear them - one of their favorite sayings being, "An old sow doesn't look like a young pig." Another "interesting person" was Billy Trays who lived near where the Marlboro library is now on 9W. The Trays family was very religious. They had many children. Billy would encourage turning to religion by writing "Jesus Saves" on various rocks and fences in the community. It is believed he would hold church services on street corners. His father was reported to have been a funeral director. If given clothes for the family they would give them away to poor people who needed them. One son, John, died a short while ago.

Cluett Schantz was also an "interesting person". Seemed he liked to pepper his language with some cuss words. Several years ago Paul Faurie in an interview had said the almost everyone in town worked for Cluett as some point. Marshall Canosa drove a feed truck for Cluett as did Bill Lyons. Unfortunately, some problems were found with the truck one day and Bill had to cool his heels in the pokey before Cluett could be called to the rescue. Cluett ran the feed store in town and his family had a feed store in Highland. Cluett became the Ulster County Sheriff. He was an avid fisherman and often would be found at the site of the town park fishing. After Cluett's death some of the townspeople approached John Quimby, who was town supervisor at that time, to name the town park in honor of Cluett Schantz.

It was cold and miserable outside. Inside, the participants were warmed, not by the flickering candle that provided little heat, but by the genuine feelings of fondness and respect that were shared in story round the "pot belly stove."

Round the Pot Belly Continued

When he took us back to Milton of the '20s and '30s Mike Canosa's eyes warmed with nostalgia. His love for the community of his childhood was very apparent. "Marlboro was half way around the world to us" he said indicating just how closely knit was his community. He took us for a memory drive down the old 9W which at that time went straight through Milton.

Mike Canosa

Conn's residence was the first in Milton (on 9W going north). Conn also had a fruit stand. Mike remembers Bob Conn as being very innovative.

Blossom Farm - had a restaurant and bar - the 4H club met at Blossom Farm. Mike remembers they had an old fashioned party where the male chose or bid for a box lunch. He was so shy, he couldn't talk to the girl. She was one of the Sears girls.

Blossom Farm
c 1940

Hepworth had the cold storage and the fruit stand went back many years. Jim Kent added, "In the beginning Hepworth had a canvass spread on trees for a stand".

Marteens had their cottages for rent - one room frame built. Mike wondered if the cottages had any water.

Marteen's Cabins
c 1938

There were fond memories of the School house - two rooms - one room for grades 1-3 and one room for grades 4-6. For 7th and 8th grade Mike went to the Sands Avenue School in Milton. For high school it was necessary to go to Highland - though Mike did spend his senior year at Marlboro. Clearly remembered was the out house out in the back and the infamous "one finger, two finger rule" when requesting permission to use the out house.

The Zellner house was old at that time. Bob Zellner recently put in his application to have the house put on the National Register.

Mom & Pa Feglia's Tea House
c 1935

Mom and Pa Feglia, on the corner of Willow Tree Road and 9W (at that time) had a "tea house" especially memorable as it had a tree growing through its roof. They also had a gas pump outside. The pump had a glass cylinder. They would fill the cylinder with however much gas you wanted and then just let gravity feed it into your car.

There was a fruit packing plant - at one time Gilmore's. Ray Shurter also had a garage in the area. The Quaker Church was where Phil Martin lives.

St. James Church - center of social activities for Mike and his family and friends. There was a recreation area across from the church. The social hall was big enough to hold basketball games. Stan Baxter remembered playing basketball there. Stan added, "It seemed very big to us, but by today's standards was really quite small".

There was a blacksmith, George Mertes, on the right - opposite the Milton Engine Company (today). In his home was the telephone operation center - "She was the 911 of her time" - when Mike's mother was about to give birth they called the operator and said they needed Dr. Freston - she said, "Don't worry, I'll get him". Mike said one never made a phone call without exchanging pleasantries with her before asking her to make the connection. Mike also spoke of the joys and travails of having a "party line"

Next came an office space for Colombo trucking - they trucked fruit to NYC to the Washington Green Market - Mr. Gus Kaley was a commission agent for a NY firm.

Mike said Frances Kaley was the manager of the Milton Bank. Mike remembers going into the bank with much trepidation as he needed to borrow money to buy property near his parents on Old Indian Road. He feared many personal questions regarding how much he had in assets etc. Frances, upon reading the application asked Mike if he were "Joe Canosa's son". When Mike replied in the affirmative, Frances said, "the papers will be ready to sign shortly" - and that was it. We all mused about the differences in banking practices and getting a mortgage today.

There was a restaurant-bar, before it became Mannese's that it was believed was called, "The Greek's place"

Libonati had a shoe repair store. Farmers could buy boots and also, have their boots repaired - a necessary part of a farmer's attire

Across the street was Kaley's market - a butcher and general store

Milton House was a small guesthouse that in later years housed tenants who tended to be "down on their heels".

Loretta Spratt had a "notions" store - all the odds and ends that were necessary for the home seamstress. She also sold groceries. The store was a "chat store", and, if the men had their pot bellied stoves, the women had their Loretta Spratt's. It was necessary to shop often to keep up with the latest news in the hamlet.

There was a community house where they sold hay, oats and feed. It was not difficult to imagine it as a stage coach stop in the past. There were different level steps. The top floor had movies. Mike remembered fondly his hero was Tom Mix with his white horse. The movie projector was hand operated and the operator was very important. He had to have a steady hand on the projector otherwise the movies would jump up and down.

The men had a social club there. They played cards and had boxing matches - bare knuckles fights as Mike remembers. Mike LaPolla was the local champ. One day someone brought a professional boxer from Poughkeepsie to fight LaPolla. When they faced each other in the ring, the professional boxer showed his training by dancing all over the ring. In exasperation Mike asked him "Did you come to fight or to dance?" Though this pithy question was remembered, the victor in the bout was not.

Dan Abbruzzi had a barber shop and Chris Miller operated a grocery store. It is believed Miller's store at one time was owned by "Rick Bourne" a company which also owned a grocery store in Marlboro and perhaps other sites. "A real chain store" Mike commented.

There was a drug store south of the library that also had an ice cream counter. That was quite the convening spot especially during the summer. Many of the guesthouse owners would meet and pick up the tourists here, just after the tourists had alighted from the Day Boat at the dock. Mike reminded us of the Mary Powell and the place she played in Milton's history. "We were a river town" he said.

Curtis Northrup was the mailman and someone suggested at one time delivered mail via horse and buggy. Carl Rhodes had a garage on the corner of Sand's Avenue.

Others chimed in with the following information. On the north corner Parrott tended the Post Office in the building. There was a bakery underneath. Booth had a hardware store. A barrel factory/cooper was across from Rhoades' garage. North of the library Dave and Cap Stenson had an eatery. "White Pants Tony" was the man to talk to if you desired liquor - he knew where all the liquor in town was available.

Mike Canosa has been a long and faithful participant in our community. For a number of years Mike was our town supervisor. He has enriched us all with his memories of the people, places and events that have shaped our "village life". Mike has given much to the community and now he gives even more as he shares his memories "round the pot belly stove".

Tying Up Loose Ends

Just thought I'd update you on several articles that have been published in the Southern Ulster Times...

From "Round the Pot Belly Stove" - Mike Canosa's dad had one of the first tvs in the area. Mike remembers the Collins Kids coming down to his house to see "Howdy Doody"

Adele Lyons - mentioned that her husband Fred Woolsey was JP in Marlborough for 14 years. She said they were "interesting" years.

On doctors in Marlborough - particularly Dr. Harris, Dr. Palmer and Dr. Scott

Adele Woolsey Lyons

One night Adele Lyons (Woolsey at the time) got a call that Irma Greene was "passed out and not breathing" - she called Dr. Scott. It was 1 a.m. in the morning - Dr. Scott headed out. On going into the house Adele smelled something and realized they were heating the house with coal. She instructed them to open the windows - Irma was suffering from coal gas poisoning. Dr. Scott said it was the quick action of opening the windows that probably saved her life. We discussed how doctors showed great concern for the patients "back then". Dr. Scott came out in the middle of the night. Dr. Harris did the same when on a snowy night he was called to tend a woman about to give birth. After taking his insulin shot he started to put on his boots. His wife chided him and said because of the bad weather, he probably wouldn't be able to make it all the way up the mountain where the woman was. Dr. Harris replied that she was his patient and needed him and he would go. Howard Quimby reported that it was not unusual for Dr. Palmer to stay all night at a patient's home if he were needed.

There was mention of a traveling doctor in Milton - one had actually set up in a tent in a field in back of Carl Rhoades'.

1888 - the year of the Blizzard - Fred Woolsey Sr. once told of burrowing a tunnel to get out. Jim Kent said George DuBois had reported the same.

Stan Baxter reported there was a harness maker - Fred Strobe who had a shop near Amadeo's in Marlboro. - then Baxter's Feed Store, a shoe store, a restaurant, a variety store and Postel's hardware store

Stan remembers in Feb. of 1953 he was attending a movie in the Marlboro theater. They smelled smoke and found that the store next to the Movie was burning - burned to the ground. This is presently the Pizza Town parking lot.

The McCourts had a Drug Store in town.

The Baxter feed store closed in 1952.

Dave Staples was unable to attend but sent some Dec 7th memories - he was piloting a plane at the time the story broke over the radio about the attack on Pearl Harbor - all flights were ordered out of the sky. He landed near Newark, NJ. In order to get home, he had to report to the nearest FBI office and get clearance to take off for the return trip.

Gerard Purdy sent the following - Trapping in Marlboro - Gerard would put out as many as 60 traps. In a good year a trapper could make $500. There was a woman by the name of Helen Sanders who had the reputation of being an excellent trapper. The real prize was trapping a Golden Muskrat - they brought the highest price of all.

From "Ice Skating on the Hudson"

It was reported that Gerard Purdy remembers ice skating from Marlborough down to Newburgh to go to the movies. After seeing the film, he would take the train back to Marlborough.

From "The Armstrongs"

Got a note from Dennis McCourt -

"I found your article on the Armstrong's last week very interesting and enlightening. I just thought you might be interested to know that the original mantelpiece from their home now resides in my living room. I purchased it from Millie Starin about 30 years ago when the Armstrong house was being torn down and Pam and I were planning on building our house. There was also a beautiful barn on the property with gigantic hand hewn beams. This also went under the bull dozer, however I was able to save some of the blacksmith made hinges from the barn doors."

"The Chimney Corner"
by David Maitland Armstrong
painted at Danskammer

Courtesy Gomez Mill House

From "Music to my Ears"

I had written about some of the musicians from Marlboro High School and mused about the whereabouts of Jack Ferguson. Lo and behold out of the blue I got a call from --- yes, Jack Ferguson. He is presently living outside of Saratoga, NY. He had gotten the story from young Joe Abbruzzi. Seems Joe's mother, Ellen Abbruzzi, subscribes to the Southern Ulster Times to keep in touch with the folks from Marlborough.

Joe Abbruzzi was the son of Dan Abbruzzi who for many years had a barber shop in Milton. Joe had served in W.W.II and had been wounded at the battle to Tinian Island. When Joe returned to Milton, he established the Tinian Tavern which he ran for a number of years. Joe then went in business with his brother-in-law, Pat Mataraza, in Pat's Diner which originally stood where the present Stewarts now stands on 9W in Milton. Pat was a Justice of the Peace in Marlborough for many years as well as a member of the School Board.

Waitressing at Pat's Diner was one of my first jobs while I was going to college. I always said Joe was my first and best boss. He was a gruff son of a gun, but had a heart of gold. I remember once, one of his steadiest customers coming to find Joe mopping out the men's room. Joe probably had about six or eight employees at the time. The customer questioned Joe whether mopping out the men's room was the "bosses' job". Joe said, "Whatever it takes." That was Joe and he earned the respect of anyone who knew him.

Jack Ferguson made a surprise visit to "the 53ers" at their December luncheon meeting at the Brick House in Marlborough.

The 53ers at Brick House
Irene Schlessinger Stevens, Camille Affuso, Jack Ferguson

Right Church - Wrong Pew

It was Betsy (Hutchins) Wilklow who first got me started researching James Monroe Taylor. I don't think he was born in Marlboro, but he was raised here on the Truncali farm. After leaving Marlboro, he was to become the President of Vassar College in Poughkeepsie (in 1886). I had learned that his mother was related to the Reverend Perkins, an early pastor at the Lattingtown Baptist Church. How long had his family been in Marlboro?

You can imagine my glee when I came across an ad on E/Bay for an original New York Times from 1879. The ad mentioned that there was an obituary of a Taylor, a resident of Milton, NY and a veteran of the war of 1812. How pleased I was when I was notified that I had won the bid (not too expensive) and the paper would be sent to me. There couldn't be too many original pages of an 1879 New York Times around. I awaited its arrival with enthused anticipation. Several days later it arrived. It took quite a bit of searching to find it as it was only a small section of the paper.

Sure enough, the headline read, "Death of a Veteran of 1812". Anxiously, I read on, "Capt. George W. Taylor of the town of Milton , in Saratoga County, died suddenly at Little Falls yesterday." SARATOGA COUNTY? 'Twas then I realized, they were writing about the "other" Milton, NY.

Foolish me, I had previously known about the other Milton, as anyone who checks finds out. There is also Marlborough in almost every state in the Union and a Marlboro in CN., MA., NH, NJ, VT, and a Marlboro County in SC as well as Marlboro in Canada and Guyana.

Thought it might be interesting to do a Google search for Milton, NY. Apparently, I'm not the only one with some orientation problems. They did list a Milton, NY with some of the following facts:

Population (2002): 17,103 with 8,559 males and 8,544 females
Median resident age: 34.0 years
Median household income: $45,262 (2000)
Median house value: $106.600 (2000)

Please note, it is not possible to define exactly the boundaries of the hamlet of Milton in the Town of Marlborough, therefore data for the Town of Milton and the Town of Marlborough have been compared.

For Marlborough, there was the following listings:

Population (2000): 8,263 with 4064 males and 4,199 females
Median resident age: 37.0 years
Median household income: $49,788 (2000)
Median house value: $142,600 (2000)
(all figures from <www.city_data.com>)

Checking the town history (Milton) one finds quite a few similarities. The original Patent was granted by the English in 1708 - the next year, Marlborough's first Patent - the Barbarie Patent was granted. (There are indications that Marlborough was settled shortly before this.) The town of Milton contains 22,000+ acres and forms a nearly perfect square. Marlborough has 14,300 acres (according to Woolsey - "History of the Town of Marlborough") and is almost a rectangle. The first roads in Milton were Native American trails - we have Old Indian Road as well as other roads to the river that were probably first forged by Native Americans. The early settlers in Milton constructed homesteads, saw and grist mills, limestone quarries and kilns - Marlborough had several of each. Milton was first known as Mill Town and in 1792 established by the state as the town of Milton. Marlborough became an official town in 1788.

Hallock's Mill - "Our" Milton

Old Mill at Town of Milton

In the early 1900s the Town of Milton saw its mills and businesses closing or moving for various reasons while improved roads and highways developed the potential for the area to become predominantly residential with workers now able to commute to nearby cities for employment. There was a similar development in the town of Marlborough.

The information continues that Milton shows continued concern to provide for its residents with - good roads, enlarged town park, summer youth recreation program, community center, senior housing and Family Fun Days. Sound familiar? It would indeed be interesting to compare the minutes of their town meetings with those of our town board.

Probably the part that impressed me most was:

"An approved Comprehensive Master Plan is taking Milton into the 21st century with vision that provides for planned growth while preserving rural and recreation areas throughout the town and along our historically significant... "Old Mill Stream"".

The above line could have easily been written by our town board.

Under the information for the Town or Milton are listed several links, some of which are for: Prospect Hill Orchards (our Milton),

River Hill Bed and Breakfast (our Milton), and Milton Elementary (our Milton). The map is for Milton, NY (the other Milton), yet the zip code given is "12547" (our Milton).

The Town Supervisor for the Town of Milton is listed as Frank D Thompson. One can only wonder what would happen if, someone using this information from the web, sent an official document to: Frank D Thompson, Supervisor, Milton, NY 12547. One can only wonder if our Supervisor, has ever run into that problem.

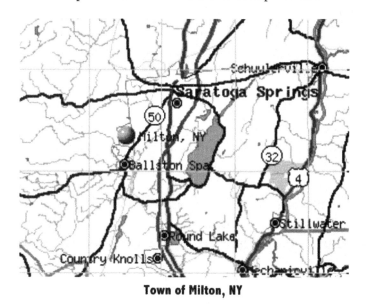

Town of Milton, NY

The "Other" Milton

It's too bad I can't use the information about Taylor that was written in the New York Times in 1879. He had been a member of the crew of the American sloop of war, "Hornet", which was at the capture of the British ship, "Peacock" in 1813. He was assigned to the task of removing the wounded prisoners from the Peacock which was sinking at the time. He was lucky to have gotten out alive.

Early on, our Milton was most often called Milton-on-the-Hudson. That has such a romantic charm - I, for one, would welcome the opportunity to wax nostalgic and once again call our hamlet "Milton-on-the-Hudson".

Yes, Virginia

Surely, most of the readers are familiar with the story of Virginia O'Hanlon. When Virginia was eight year old in 1897, plagued with doubts, she asked her father if there really was a Santa Claus. Since it was family tradition that whenever questions of language usage or history came up, a letter was written to *The New York Sun*, her father advised her, "If you see it in *The Sun*, it's so." She then wrote a letter to the editor and shortly thereafter the editorial was printed.

"Yes, Virginia, there is a Santa Claus. He exists as certainly as love and generosity and devotion exist, and you know that they abound and give to your life its highest beauty and joy...."

This was to become one of the most memorable editorials in newspaper history.

This is but one indication of the power of the printed word. When lacking an official birth certificate, the hand written entries in a family bible have been recognized as legal proof. When unable to read or write, a scrawled "X" in the right spot was considered legally binding. A number of years ago, in Germany, finding an important family document, I was quite pleased. I told the archivist that I had been searching for this for a number of years. He replied, "Paper is patient". If, today, one has a problem, in order to get relief, it is necessary to "put it in writing". Most recently Dan Rather, in a controversial TV report relied on written documentation.

Thus you can imagine my mental salivation when I saw the following in print:

"After passing several small villages up the river, the village of Marlborough is interesting in that it is a pre-Revolutionary village and was the capital of the State of New York for a short time" This was found while I was browsing the shelves in the library of the Historical Society of Newburgh Bay and Highlands. The book, *The Hudson River Today and Yesterday*, written by Arthur P Abbott was published in 1915 by the Historian Publishing Co. NYC. (Eat your heart out Kingston)

Of course, when speaking of the New York State Capital "for a short time" he was referring to Kingston, not Marlborough, however it is IN PRINT!

Included in the book was this picture of the Marlboro river front (in 1915)

Let's hope 90+ years from now (2095) nobody says, "Marlboro was once the capital of New York, I read it in the *Southern Ulster Times.*

Bare Feet, Stubbed Toes and the Wood pile
by Valeria Dawes Terwilliger

Part of being poor in the depression years was owning only one pair of shoes at a time. You took very good care of that pair and often wore it beyond its normal fit. Another year older might mean another pair of shoes, if your feet grew substantially. These shoes were worn daily in all seasons, except during the summer months. After school was out in June, they were never put on, except for Church or Sunday School. Anyway, in September they were pretty tight, for whatever reason. Hopefully, you might manage to have a new pair to celebrate "back to school."

Valeria Dawes Terwilliger

Bingham Road that went by our house was a dirt road. In the spring, the "road men" came along with machines, rakes and shovels and they scratched it up and raked it over and then rolled it all down again.

Ultimately, showers would come along to wet the dust and transform "Big Hill" into piles of pebbles, stones and gullies. It was fun to splash around in all that when it was wet, but eventually the stones and pebbles got stuck into little chunks and deposits, that did not move. Most accumulations were in the middle or along the edges of the road. Since "Big Hill" was the mail artery to most all of the doings of the family farm, it seemed that you were always walking (or running) up or down. By midsummer the bottoms of my shoeless feet had toughened up to come close to resembling the shoe leather that should have covered them. However, with all the use and abuse these feet got, somehow the big toe never toughened up enough to survive the abuse part. While running up and down the hill, it was really a good and quite unusual day if I didn't stub my toe against a rock. Pebbles and stones though they were, I remember them best as rocks, because the pain seemed endless. Ultimately, I'd crack my toe again, before it had healed. We had no band-aids of course, so a white rag tied around the toe would last only a short time, before it was bloody and dirty or it fell off altogether. Unfortunately, the stones on "Big Hill" were only one of the many hazards to bare feet. The raspberry patch, where we picked berries 6 days a week, was full of stones and pebbles too, not to mention the fallen raspberry branches, which were full of treacherous stickers too. My poor feet!!!

Being the youngest and smallest in the family, I was given chores that I could do and that the others didn't want to do. One of these was keeping the box behind our kitchen stove filled with firewood. This stove was not only used to cook the daily meals and to can fruit and vegetables for winter use, but it also provided heat for the entire house. So, let me tell you that getting in the wood was a very important and endless job. I didn't use a basket or bucket, because that much wood would have been too heavy for me to carry. Instead, I just picked up four or five sticks as carefully as possible in my arms and headed for the house. Now the problem was to accomplish all this in bare feet. You had to make really sure you weren't going to drop a piece, because it ultimately would end up on your toe or entire foot. In the woodpile, sticks had a way of getting stuck under each other, so as a very last resort you might climb around on the pile to find sticks that you could move. You always could count on a stick rolling onto or over your toes and feet.

Horrors!!! I still can feel it now. This means of torture was probably not invented as such, but it would have been very persuasive indeed.

Eventually, after rubber was no longer salvaged and saved for the WWII effort, shoes became more available for those with money and rationing points to buy them. However, I can remember people holding the soles of their shoes on with jar rubbers, when they couldn't purchase new shoes in the stores. Thankfully, I escaped that fate, but perhaps that would have been a good idea, especially when approaching the woodpile.

Forefathers' Rock

Plymouth in Massachusetts is justly proud of their being the landing place of the Pilgrims in 1620. The site is marked with a rock engraved to memorialize the momentous occasion. Regrettably, there's no historical record of any connection between the actual Pilgrims and the actual rock.

How many people are aware that Marlborough, too, could have its "Forefathers' Rock"? One of the early settlers in town was Edward Hallock, who braved the winter weather of 1760 with his family of wife and twelve children. The text Our Quaker Forebears, edited by Theodora M Carrell (available at the Milton Library), records the recollections of Nathaniel Hallock, grandson of Edward. "I remember no stories of the leave-taking or embarkation, but was told that in his early life, having owned and commanded a trading vessel, and still living by the sea, Hallock could not have lived without a water craft of some kind."

According to Cochrane's 1887 History of the Town of Marlborough, Edward Hallock was the first of his name to settle within the precinct of Marlborough. He was a descendant of Peter Hallock, one of the flock of the Pilgrims who located with Rev. John Young in Connecticut in 1640. Edward brought his family from Long Island and came to Milton. According to Cochrane, the party landed on a rock which was known as "Forefathers' Rock" and bears the inscription "E. Hallock 1760." "The old landmark stands on land now owned by Christopher Champlin (NB in 1887) on the line of the West Shore Railroad."

Woolsey's 1908 <u>History of Marlborough</u> mentions the rock as follows: "On December 31, 1760, Edward Hallock, a Friends' minister from Long Island, with his family, landed his sloop a short distance south of Milton at a rock known as Forefathers' Rock and marked 'E. H.'"

That's the good news, now here's the bad. John Matthews in an article entitled <u>Marlboro Country of the Mid-Hudson</u> says "The Hallocks have an account of their ancestors' arrival, and landing at what was called Forefathers' Rock, which rock was destroyed when the West Shore Railroad was built."

If there is anyone out there with the pioneering spirit, our town supervisor, Tom Coupart, (NB in 2003) would love to have someone find and dig up the rock. He says he'll donate the shovel. Just check with him.

Wouldn't it be wonderful to have our own Forefathers' Rock back?

THE ICEMAN WENTETH!

How convenient things are now. Sometimes, in the hectic ebb and flow of our lives we forget how easy things can be. We can shop on the internet, or go to our usual stores where we can buy such luxuries as fresh lettuce and bright red tomatoes even in the dead of winter. Seldom do we think of what our parents and grandparents had to do just to keep up their normal existences. Sometimes, going back brings a realization and a respect for their ingenuity. One such reminder is to consider how our antecedents kept their food fresh considering there was no refrigeration. I would dare to guess that there are a number of people still living who remember the window box - where there was a shelf or box on the outside of the window in which perishables would be put to keep them cold. This, of course, only worked when the weather outside was cold enough. Or, better yet, the ice box. To his dying day my uncle called any refrigerator an "icebox". An ice box was more convenient than a window box, because you could keep things cold no matter what the weather - as long as you had ice. The ice box was just that - shaped like our refrigerator of today, it had one section to hold the block of ice, one section for the food, and a pan at the bottom called the drip pan to catch the water as the ice melted. Dumping the ice pan was an arduous chore as chances were good you would end up splashing the cold water on yourself. Knowing that warm air rises and cold air falls, our ancestors were wise enough to put the ice section at the top.

An ice box worked out well - except - it had to be continually filled with new ice as the old ice melted away. Now to get ice, we either check our freezers, or pick some up at the local store. There are a good number of stores that carry ice - in bags - in a freezer either inside the store or just outside the door. Back some time ago that was not the case. Ice, at least in the warmer months, was not easy to get. It was not made but rather was harvested - from local ponds during the frigid part of the winter.

J.C.Wygant taking ice from the pond

There is an excellent description of harvesting ice in the text, "Early in the Morning" by Marion Edey ne Armstrong of the DansKammer Armstrong family. She tells of her and her brother accompanying the local butcher to Middle Pond where there were men already working on getting blocks of ice. They used a horse to pull the "ice marker" - "something like a mowing machine with two enormous knives underneath" which dug deep into the ice, marking it off into blocks. From there, men with saws - "their double ice saw - scrape-scrape, scrape-scrape, like rusty music" would cut the ice through. On one side was a channel of water through which the block of ice was floated using a pole with a spike to guide it. The big cakes of ice were shoved along the channel to the place where another man with a hook was hauling them out of the water. They were then loaded into a horse-drawn wagon to be taken to the ice house.

In Marlborough there were several families that harvested ice when their fruit trees gave them a respite from their usual farming. One family was the Wygant family. (John) Calvin, son of Clemence, was born in 1863. In 1890 he married Charlotte Barnes and was given, by his father Clemence, land that he developed between Western Avenue and Church Street in Marlborough. He built his house (presently Esposito's home) and a barn and an icehouse. There was also a tennis court. He ran a small farm there.

The Wygant ice house in back of the family residence on Church Street

Now, the ice house was a specialty building. There were a few in Marlborough. An icehouse usually was a rectangular building - often with no or very small windows. The icehouse would be "insulated" with straw or saw dust. In this case insulated, not to keep the cold out, but to keep the cold in. The blocks would often be buried in straw or

166

saw dust. The Wygant icehouse was destroyed in the 1905 fire that also consumed the barn.

Marion, was the daughter of J Calvin Wygant. In the 1960s she wrote some memoirs in which she told of the day when "she and a cousin went to the forbidden icehouse to get some apples to eat. They located the apples, buried in sawdust, by lighting matches. That night the icehouse and the barn burned. She strongly suspected that she knew the reason."

Another ice-harvester and farmer was John Manion. He reaped his ice from the pond near the Marlboro High School called, "Manion's Pond". At one end of the pond was the icehouse - near where there was a small waterfall.

In a 1983 8th grade assignment Joe Caserto interviewed John Manion. Later he quoted -

Mr. Manion's first job was bringing ice to the refrigerated railroad cars. 'The ice business was a good one because there were no refrigerators,' said Mr. Manion. The ice came from the pond on his property. It is called Manion's pond. They would supply all the small farms. The ice was about twelve inches thick and would be cut with a plow. After being cut it would be lifted with a bar, put on a horse and wagon, and delivered. Because farmers had no work in the winter, they were eager to work for the Manions. 'For twenty five cents an hour you could hire all the men you wanted!'

Manion ice house courtesy Jim Manion

The icehouse kept the ice frozen during the Spring, Summer and hopefully through the Fall. The ice was then available to individual families to stow in their iceboxes. Often there was an iceman who would bring a wagon of ice along a specified route to sell the ice to individual homes, or people would go to the icehouse and the owner would retrieve a block or two of ice for them which they then paid for.

Yes, it is so much easier now. Many refrigerators have automatic ice makers insuring the household never runs out of ice. Some refrigerators have an outlet in the door by which one can get a glassful of ice for whatever beverage is to be consumed.

Yes, things are easier.

Does anyone long for those crisp winter mornings, the snorting of the horses carting the wagon, the marking of the ice, "the scrape-scrape, scrape-scrape, like rusty music" of the saws, the loading of the ice into the sweet smelling icehouse? Does anyone remember getting some of the slivers or scrapings off the blocks of ice and putting the cool, thirst-quenching melting ice into the mouth and feeling as if it were a special treat? Ah, progress!!!

Manion icehouse - watercolor by Ellen Esposito - courtesy of the artist

The Iceman Wenteth - Cont.

You thought we were done! So did I. The last story was written about Ice Harvesting in Marlborough with information about the Manion Ice House and the Wygant Ice House. After the story was written, I came across other information that was just too juicy to not share. For the last story, I had met with Jim Manion. He sent me to see his sister, Judy Gephard who Jim said still had a number of the original tools used in the cutting and storing of ice.

Judy and her husband, Bill were great. They took me to their storage and one by one we pulled these wonderful old tools out into the sunshine. We didn't know all that we looked at and were quite surprised when one tool, as we dragged it out, had the wooden sheathing moved back to give us a glimpse of the Ice Plow.

Manion Ice Plow

The Ice Plow was used to score the ice more deeply making it easier for the Ice Saws to do their work. The Spud was used to separate the ice blocks. The most treasured article was the hook that the Gephards kept in their home. It was a hook that was placed over a beam in the ice house and used as a sort of pulley to raise and lower the blocks of ice. There were a lot of tools. We laughed as we tried to figure out how the "mystery tool" was used.

Bill Gephard and Ice Saw

Checking with Plank (History of the Town of Marlborough, 1959, p18) we find he says, "The long building most recently occupied by the Fruit Exchange was, if we are not mistaken, once an icehouse of the Knickerbocker Ice Company." The Knickerbocker Ice Company dominated the ice business in the late 1800s. The major market was New York City, but they also shipped domestically to places such as New Orleans and Charleston and internationally to India and the Caribbean. The ice companies had two methods of transporting the ice to their customers - the first was via large barges in the Hudson River, the second was to load the ice onto railcars and ship the ice via rail.

Checking deeds one discovers in 1925 land was sold to the Hudson Valley Refrigerating Co. down near the Marlborough dock. In 1972 there was a deed to the Marlboro Freezers, Inc. Were they involved in the ice harvesting business?

It was interesting to find another ice house in Marlboro, right on Western Avenue. The Old House Survey (1968) mentions the ice house of JC and GH Milden. According to that text the Milden brothers used this house for an icehouse and had a dam behind it on Old Man's Creek, presumably their source of ice.

A deed from 1874 shows almost 8 acres going to Jacob B and George H Milden on Old Man's Creek in Marlboro. The Mildens were an old, respected African American family of Marlborough. We read in Cochrane, "J. C. & G. H. Milden have a livery stable, and do all kinds of teaming and hauling, and run a stage in the summer season. They also cut ice from Milden's pond in the winter, and deliver to owners of small ice houses."

According to the Old House Survey, in 1930 the ice house was purchased by Alan Purdy who removed the top story and made it a house. Purdy then took off another story and then a third story leaving only one story to the house. In 1968 the house was owned by Theo Partington.

Milden "Ice House"

Seeing the Milden ice house brought back memories of another iceman in Marlboro, Jesse Elliott. I was able to meet with Jesse, Jr. and his wife, Carol. Jesse said his father had taken over the Manion customers when Manion gave up the business. He thought his father used first the Manion ice house. He remembers his father's truck falling through the ice on Manion's pond. Later Elliott built a small ice house next to his garage. Jesse Jr. also had a few of the old ice tools. One of his prizes is an ice pick labeled on four sides: 1) Jesse Elliott, 2) Phone Marlboro 199, 3) Marlborough, NY, and 4) ice - coal- wood. Note the phone number 199 is later than the "75" on the Manion advertisement. Jesse, Jr. thinks his father gave out these ice picks as advertisement.

Jesse Elliott, Jr. & ice pick

Interestingly, when the ice man came, often he was armed only with a cloth or leather pad that he threw over his shoulder and ice tongs that gripped onto the block of ice. The ice man would bring the ice into the home. The icebox usually was in the kitchen. The usual pleasantries were generally exchanged with various members of the family. Thus the ice man became an important link in the community often carrying the "news of the day", or the gossip. Some people picked their ice up at the ice house. That meant a quick trip home so the ice didn't melt. Every family had in its possession at least one ice pick with which to cut the large block of ice. Do you still have an ice pick in your home?

What fun it has been for me to discover the important place ice harvesting had in Marlborough's history. Hope you've enjoyed also.

The Quadricentennial
Half Moon

During the Fall of 2008, the replica of the Half Moon docked for a week at the Newburgh dock. It was open for visitors to board the ship and find out about the sailing conditions of the original Half Moon in 1609. Henry Hudson sailing for the Dutch was the first European credited with sailing up the river that was to bear his name. During 2009 there are to be various programs planned to commemorate this event.

Each of the fourth grade classes within the Marlborough School District were privileged to tour the Half Moon. Boy Scout Troop #72 also had the opportunity of visiting the ship and learning of the history involved in that voyage.

Milton Historic Tour

One of the activities of the Town of Marlborough for the Quad-ricententennial was the Milton Historic Tour which commenced on Saturday May 2, 2009 sponsored by the Friends of the Historic Milton-on-the Hudson Train Station.

A later writing stated, "Saturday was "Opening Day" for the Historic Trail of the Hamlet of Milton. Sandwiched between days filled with rain, the weather cooperated for a perfect day to walk, drive or cruise in a stroller along a loop beginning and ending at the Town owned, Milton-on-Hudson Train Station! Participants in this ExploreNY and Town of Marlborough Quadricentennial event were able to clearly see the historical connection between the river and family and commercial lives in and around the hamlet of Milton."

The Friends had prepared a lovely catalog of the various stops along the Historic Trail.

Milton-on-Hudson Train Station

Built 1883; is a significant landmark of an era important to the Hudson River Valley. Standing at the foot of the Farmers' Turnpike, it was the center of commerce in the town for many years with farmers bringing their produce to, first the dock and then the train station for shipment to places around the world. Nearby was the dock for the Mary Powell, famous steamboat.

(see previous)

Hudson River Fruit Exchange

Between 400 & 500 farmers on the west bank of the Hudson were allied in a cooperative business known as the Hudson River Fruit Exchange, George Hildebrand was the General Manager of the HR Fruit Exchange and Cold Storage.

Warehouse, main office and cold storage at Milton

175

Woolsey Building

Built by C. Meech Woolsey in 1896. Woolsey was born in 1841 in Lattingtown. Woolsey was town supervisor and member of the State Assembly as well as a veteran of the Civil War. He wrote the "History of the Town of Marlborough" in 1908. This building contained Woolsey's law office, the first library in Milton, the post office, and the jailhouse.

Presbyterian Church

In 1842 the Presbyterians purchased land from Jonathon Kent at the intersection of Church St and North Road and built their first church there. In 1899 that property was exchanged with Mary Conklin for property at the current site.

First Presbyterian Church   Milton, NY 12547

The Milton Presbyterian Church on Church Street was built in 1800.
From 2005 calendar Marlborough Historical Society

Milton Methodist Church and Cemetery

Oldest Methodist Church in Ulster County. Congregation began in 1786 when Ezekiel Cooper a circuit rider from New Jersey conducted services at the home of John Woolsey. This structure built in 1812, improvements were made 1855, 1904, and 1905. The original entrance was at the East end.

Java Head

Built circa 1850; Summer home of Raphael Weed, noted artist and historian. Weed created the homecoming gift for Admiral Dewey after Dewey's victorious action in the Spanish American War in Manilla in 1898. He was President of the Newburgh Historical Society and helped gain recognition of the fact that American Nation as a Republic was born in Newburgh.

Former Button Factory Sands Dock Family Compound

Second Sands Homestead. Built circa 1820. Built with character and "a touch of elegance" (as per Perry Kent).

Gervais House ~ Newman House

Lots #49 and #50 on the map of the estate of David Sands 1859. Once owned by John Newman. Newman bought the Wheel Barrow Factory on the waterfront next to the train station from Sumner Coleman. The New York Gazeteer published in 1860, reported that the plant was turning out 40,000 wheelbarrows a year at that time. Premises also owned by Clement Gervais at one time and, at a later time, by the Milton Church of the Resurrection .

Cherry Hill School - no longer standing

Property bought in 1858 from the Estate of David Sands. The school had a small hall for the boys and another for the girls. Contained about 150 desks, Had a long platform upon which the students stood when reciting their lessons. A large round stove was in the center. A teacher of note was Hattie Dickenson, her reputation was formidable. Was replaced in 1937 by the Milton Elementary School.

(see previous)

All Saints Episcopal Church

Organized in 1850 as a Mission of Christ Church, Marlboro with the Rector, the Rev Samuel Hawksley. The cornerstone was laid in 1854, completed 1856, first services held 1857. Used during summers mid-1940 & 1950's for migrant workers church services under the auspices of the Methodist, Episcopal and Presbyterian Churches. Also served as the Milton Grange Hall

Tristram Coffin House

Tristram Coffin wrote "The Lost Gold Mine of the Hudson" Written in 1915, the story keeps alive and embellishes the often told and retold legends of mystery and treasure. His description of the small hamlet of "knotlimb" is a thinly veiled reference to Milton
(See previous)

Samuel Hallock House

A log house was built at this site about 1740 which afterward became a part of this small frame house, being the north part. Remains much the same as when built with two stone fireplaces. Probably the oldest standing house in Marlborough. Fired on by the British in 1777, Samuel Hallock rowed out to chastise the British.

Anning Smith House

The first part of this house was built by Leonard Smith in the early 1700s. His son, Anning Smith was a lieutenant in the Revolutionary Army. In 1777 as Vaughn's expedition sailed up the Hudson to burn Kingston, shots were fired on this house. The cemetery on the property is one of the oldest in town and is the final resting place of Native Americans as well as members of the Smith family. Also buried here is Peleg Ransome, a Revolutionary War soldier.

Anning Smith

Sarah Hull Hallock Library

Endowed by Sarah Hull Hallock who died in 1884. Trustees were appointed and from 1896 to 1924 the library was housed in the Woolsey Bjuilding. Sarah Hull Hallock was very prominent in the Woman's Suffrage movement and admired by Susan B. Anthony.

Mannese - Miller Dry Goods

C Jacob Miller, came to Milton from Germany in 1866 and opened a barber shop and cigar store. On the 1871 list of landholders Christopher Jacob Miller is listed as hair dresser and dealer in cigars. He sold the land in 1924. The property was purchased in 1944 by Joseph and Pauline Mannese and has been in the Mannese family since as a restaurant.

St. James Roman Catholic Church

Organized in 1865 as a mission from Rosendale. The building dedicated in 1877. Father Mee, pastor who also served the Marlborough church, was instrumental in buying the land for the cemetery on Lattingtown Road. In 1974 Cardinal Cook helped plant a dogwood on the occasion of the hundredth anniversary of the church.

Innes (Inness) Barn

Built circa 1770. The big barn was used for several years by the famous Hudson River School artist, George Innes, who summered in the Hull and Hallock boarding house across the road. Innes was born in 1825. He painted some of his best known pictures from his studio in the haymow in the early 1880s.

Zellner House

Built circa 1770; got the name of 'Washington's Headquarters' because legend has it that George Washington stopped here and the local COMMITTEE OF SAFTEY met here during the Revolutionary War. Believed to have been an early stage stop.

The Captain William Bond House/ later Ed Hallock House - no longer existing

Built in 1730 by William Bond, a sea captain and original patentee. Given to his daughter Sukie, it came into possession of Ed Hallock by 1760's. Edward Hallock and family of ten children lived one whole winter here. The first Friends meetings were held here.

Hull/Hallock House

In 1861 Nathaniel Hallock deeded this property to Sarah Hull Hallock, widow of Edward Hallock, and Dorcus Hull, her sister. The sisters set up a boarding house that became a beacon for intellectuals and activists. They had visitors who included: George Innes, Susan B Anthony, Frederick Douglas.

Elverhoj Art Colony (Private)

Built by Sherburne Sears, a whaling captain, circa 1840. Purchased by Anders Anderson in 1912 and designed as a summer retreat and workshop for arts and crafts . It has a Moorish terrace overlooking the Hudson River which became a popular restaurant post WWI . In the 1930s was Elverhoj Summer Theatre, one of the first dinner theaters. It was sold to Father Devine in 1938 and became one of his havens on the Hudson.

Ship Lantern Inn

Mr. Foglia is one of the four original founders of the renouned Chef-Boy-Ar-Dee Company which was awarded the Army and Navy "E" as a result of sample tastings supplied from the kitchen of this restaurant. Ship Lantern Inn is now enjoying its third generation of family management.

Friends of Progress Cemetery (Willow Tree)

Earliest Quaker cemetery in Marlborough. Land conveyed to the Society of Friends about 1780 by Elijah Lewis, resting place of the Ketchem Brothers, Civil War Quaker soldiers and many other noted Quakers. "As much as they hated WAR, they hated SLAVERY more"

Ketchem House ("the Mill House") - no longer standing

Built next to a Hallock Mill; birthplace of the Ketchem Brother, the Quaker soldiers of the Civil War, both killed, buried across the street in the Friends Cemetery. Now these lands are part of the Cluett Schantz town park. Cluett Schantz was former town supervisor and Ulster County Sheriff.

Nathaniel Hallock House

Built in the early 1800s. Birthplace of Mary Hallock Foote. Foote was born into a Quaker family that fostered female accomplishment. She became one of the foremost female illustrators of the American West in the late 19th and early 20th century. This house appeared in architectural magazines. Before the change in highways (in the mid 1930s) there was a gravity flow of water into the house and in fountains outdoors.

(see previous)

Friends Cemetery (near Hallock Pond Watson Ave)

Circa 1830, Foster Hallock transferred to the Society of Friends (Marlborough Monthly Meeting). This is the second Quaker cemetery in Marlborough and became a necessity by the riving of the Quakers into two groups. The rift was caused by doctrinal differences between the Orthodox and the Hicksite factions.

Friends Meeting House/School

In 1804 Joshua Sutton deeded land south of Milton and on the east side of the post road to James Hallock, John Wood and Samuel Adams, trustees of the Quaker meeting. A meeting house was built and occupied until 1828 when the rift between the Orthodox and Hicksite Quakers caused the Orthodox Quakers to seek another site for a meeting house.

Friends Church

Friends School

Hallock Mill (Watson Ave)

Built by the Hallock family. By early 1800s owned by Foster Hallock. In 1836 deeded to George Hallock. George Hallock died in 1875 and in 1894 the land was deeded to Robert W. Hallock, his son. Robert Hallock ran the mill, started by his grandfather, Foster, for many years. He died in 1927 while at work at the mill. The mill was demolished in the 1940s. Today only a chimney remains.

Foundry and Mill Pond. Milton, N.Y.

Saints' Rest

Built by George and Sarah Birdsall Hallock in 1862. Family legend indicates it was built by soldiers returning from the Civil War. It remains a lovely home and a tribute to the concept of stewardship - the careful tending of the land and its history as a gift to future generations.

Hallock House 1862
"Saint's Rest"
Milton-on- Hudson, NY.

From the Marlborough Historical Society
Calendar 2007

Life She Was Simpler Back Then!
Life, she was simpler back then!

We were just beginning to feel our oats "back then" - young teen-agers with little in personal history, but big hopes for the future. Most of the guys and a few of the gals had gotten their drivers' licenses, and, while there were the beginnings of dating, most of us went out together as a group - usually in the back of one of the boy's family pick-ups. This was probably the first unchaperoned party I had ever attended ... but then, Emma Quimby and Ruth McElrath were close at hand and anyone knowing either of the two ladies realized that neither one would have tolerated any nonsense. Then too, we were either too dull or too naive to even think of raising any eyebrows.

It was all Sabra's (Sabra McElrath Jesionek) idea. Sabra was one of those girls who loved the simpler and more wholesome activities - loved being a country girl. She had gotten permission from Emma and Sam Quimby to hold a Halloween party at the Quimby barns. She and her siblings along with the Quimby boys (Paul, Howard and Sam) had cleaned up one of the barn rooms in preparation of the big event.

As we arrived, many having been driven there by a parent, we had to walk through the barnyard to get to our destination. When we slid the barn door open to enter, we were met with a festive scene. There were a few lights in the room - mostly light bulbs hanging from wires; our seats for the evening were to be bales of hay; our dance floor, the barn floor that had been swept clean of most of the loose straw and hay.

We had just had lessons in gym class on square dancing and Sabra had hunted up some good records complete with the square dance calls. The girls came dressed in festive skirts and blouses, a number of them recently hand made. A number of the boys wore the flannel shirt of the farmer.

During the evening we were ever aware of the animals sleeping in their stalls nearby. The air was perfumed with the smell of hay and animal. There was nothing noxious about it - the smell was clean and earthy. The sounds of the animals shifting about were reminders that we were sharing their space. They probably heard us as loud and intrusive - their sounds were muffled and slow, adding to the serenity of the evening.

Refreshments were cider and doughnuts and everyone enjoyed a goodly portion of both. We did a lot of dancing, not all square dances, but enough to satisfy our "back to the farm" appetites. We also did a lot of laughing and enjoying - enjoying each other's company, enjoying being young, enjoying living in a farming community, enjoying the sharing of space with the animals, enjoying the simplicity and the beauty of the Quimby barns. They were that night, over 50 years ago, much as they are today, and much as they had been for about 100 years before that.

Back Row - Billy McElrath, Joyce Krause, Joe Casseles, Vinnie Vasile, Jack Ferguson, George Rusk, Eddie Crosby Front Row - Shirley Patterson, MaryLou Hennekens, Joan Affuso, Jeannie Greiner, Valeria Dawes, Cynthia Carpenter, Carol Anne Casseles and Sabra McElrath

Pictured are: (Back row)
Billy McElrath, (brother of Sabra),

Joyce Krauss Morris - her parents owned and ran Marteen Cabins on 9W in Milton;

Joe Casscles who is retired and lives in the town of Newburgh, Joe's and Carol Ann's grandfather was Sylvanus Casscles who for many years ran a grocery store in Marlboro;

Vinnie Vasile (deceased) who retired from IBM and lived on Bingham Road with his family - his family lived in the old Bingham homestead;

Jack Ferguson (does anyone have any news about Jack?);

George Rusk, attorney in Marlboro, George's grandfather, also an attorney settled in Marlboro in the mid 1800s;

Eddie Crosby, (deceased) also retired from IBM and lived in the town of Newburgh, one of Eddie's forebears was Levi Crosby who was a blacksmith in Lattingtown in the early 1800s;

Paul Quimby whose family has been in Marlborough since before the Revolution

(Front Row)

Shirley Patterson Koran, married Charlie a retired State Policeman and lives on 9W in Milton, Shirley's father was Felix Patterson who lived on Western Avenue in Marlboro and was foreman on Conway's farm (now a golf course) and a beekeeper;

MaryLou Hennekens Mahan, (yours truly);

Joan Affuso Fazio, retired living in Newburgh, Joan's grandfather Dominick Affuso came to Marlboro in 1911, but his mother and father were already living in town;

Jean Greiner Betters, married a US Army officer, the Greiners bought their first property in West Marlboro in 1878 and have farmed the area ever since;

Valeria Dawes Terwilliger, (Ed.D), retired from teaching, Valeria's family were in Marlboro in the early 1800s, relatives now populate "Dawesville" just over the border with Plattekill;

Cynthia Carpenter Gervais living in California, Cynthia's family goes back to Joseph Carpenter who was the first settler in Lattingtown and his stone is in the Baptist church yard there;

Carol Ann Casscles, (sister of Joseph above) is living in Connecticut; and

Sabra McElrath Jesionek presently living near Boston, Sabra's family goes back to Wm. McElrath who was in Marlboro by 1835 (then spelled McIlrath). Her mother was a Sears and traced her line back to Sherbourne Sears, a sea captain who built what later was to become the ElVerhoj art colony in Milton

As we left that night, the moon was full and bright, the air had an autumn nip. The barns and the fields behind them were bathed in moonlight and had a mystical air.

I've been to fancier soirees in the 50+ years since that night, where the ambiance was much more expensively established, the refreshments more gourmet, and the participants more urbane and renown. Yet, this remains as one of my favorite memories. I guess the old adage KISS (keep it simple, stupid) is a reminder of what truly resonates in both mind and spirit

Carol Ann Casscles and Eddie Crosby

Sabra McElrath & Paul Quimby

and Quimby barns

Index

Printed in the United States
by Baker & Taylor Publisher Services